CLASSIC SERMONS ON JESUS THE SHEPHERD

Kregel Classic Sermon Series

Classic Sermons on Angels
Classic Sermons on the Apostle Paul
Classic Sermons on the Apostle Peter
Classic Sermons on the Attributes of God
Classic Sermons on the Birth of Christ
Classic Sermons on Christian Service
Classic Sermons on the Church
Classic Sermons on the Cross of Christ
Classic Sermons on Death and Dying
Classic Sermons on Faith and Doubt
Classic Sermons on Family and Home
Classic Sermons on the Fruit of the Spirit
Classic Sermons on the Grace of God
Classic Sermons on Heaven and Hell
Classic Sermons on the Holy Spirit
Classic Sermons on Hope
Classic Sermons on Jesus the Shepherd
Classic Sermons on Judas Iscariot
Classic Sermons on Lesser-Known Bible Characters
Classic Sermons on the Lord's Prayer
Classic Sermons on the Love of God
Classic Sermons on the Miracles of Jesus
Classic Sermons on the Names of God
Classic Sermons on the Old Testament Prophets
Classic Sermons on Overcoming Fear
Classic Sermons on the Parables of Jesus
Classic Sermons on Praise
Classic Sermons on Prayer
Classic Sermons on the Prodigal Son
Classic Sermons on the Resurrection of Christ
Classic Sermons on Revival and Spiritual Renewal
Classic Sermons on the Seasons of Life
Classic Sermons on the Second Coming and Other Prophetic Themes
Classic Sermons on the Sovereignty of God
Classic Sermons on Spiritual Warfare
Classic Sermons on Stewardship
Classic Sermons on Suffering
Classic Sermons on the Will of God
Classic Sermons on the Word of God
Classic Sermons on World Evangelism
Classic Sermons on Worship

CLASSIC SERMONS ON JESUS THE SHEPHERD

Compiled by
Warren W. Wiersbe

Kregel
Academic & Professional

Classic Sermons on Jesus the Shepherd
Compiled by Warren W. Wiersbe

Published by Kregel Publications, a division of Kregel, Inc., P.O. Box 2607, Grand Rapids, MI 49501. Kregel Publications provides trusted, biblical publications for Christian growth and service. Your comments and suggestions are valued.

For more information about Kregel Publications, visit our web site at: www.kregel.com.

Cover photo: PhotoDisc

ISBN 0-8254-4105-6

Printed in the United States of America
1 2 3 4 5 / 06 05 04 03 02

Contents

List of Scripture Texts 6

Preface 7

1. The Good Shepherd: A Farewell Sermon 9
   George Whitefield

2. The Good Shepherd 27
   Frederick W. Robertson

3. The Preparation for Shepherding the Sheep 43
   George Campbell Morgan

4. The Lord Is My Shepherd 61
   James McGinlay

5. The Shepherd King of Israel 73
   Alexander Maclaren

6. The Good Shepherd 83
   Henry Parry Liddon

7. The Lord's Guests 97
   John Henry Jowett

8. The Divine Shepherd 105
   Joseph Parker

9. The Good Shepherd 113
   John A. Broadus

10. The Good Shepherd 119
    Robert Murray McCheyne

11. The Good Shepherd 127
    Henry Allan Ironside

12. The Overflowing Cup 137
    Charles Haddon Spurgeon

List of Scripture Texts

Psalm 23, Maclaren 73
Psalm 23, McGinlay 61
Psalm 23, Parker 105
Psalm 23:5, Jowett 97
Psalm 23:5, Spurgeon 137
John 10:1–6, McCheyne 119
John 10:1–16, Ironside 127
John 10:11, Broadus 113
John 10:11, Liddon 83
John 10:14–15, Robertson 27
John 10:27–28, Whitefield 9
John 21:15–17, Morgan 43

Preface

THE *Kregel Classic Sermons Series* is an attempt to assemble and publish meaningful sermons from master preachers about significant themes.

These are *sermons*, not essays or chapters taken from books about themes. Not all of these sermons could be called great, but all of them are *meaningful*. They apply the truths of the Bible to the needs of the human heart, which is something that all effective preaching must do.

While some are better known than others, all of the preachers whose sermons I have selected had important ministries and were highly respected in their day. The fact that a sermon is included in this volume does not mean that either the compiler or the publisher agrees with or endorses everything that the man did, preached, or wrote. The sermon is here because it has a valued contribution to make.

These are sermons about *significant* themes. The pulpit is no place to play with trivia. The preacher has thirty minutes in which to help mend broken hearts, change defeated lives, and save lost souls; he can never accomplish this demanding ministry by distributing homiletical tidbits. In these difficult days we do not need clever pulpiteers who discuss the times; we need dedicated ambassadors who will preach the eternities.

The reading of these sermons can enrich your spiritual life. The studying of them can enrich your skills as an interpreter and expounder of God's truth. However God uses these sermons in your life and ministry, my prayer is that His church around the world will be encouraged and strengthened by them.

—WARREN W. WIERSBE

The Good Shepherd: A Farewell Sermon

George Whitefield (1714–1770) was born in Gloucester, England, and was educated at Pembroke College, Oxford. There he came under the influence of John Wesley and Charles Wesley, although Whitefield was more Calvinistic in doctrine than they. Ordained in the Anglican Church, he quickly gained a reputation as an effective preacher, but the Anglican churches disapproved of him because of his association with the Methodists. He began to preach to great crowds out-of-doors and led John Wesley to follow his example. Whitefield made seven visits to America and is recognized in American history as a leader of evangelism and spiritual awakening.

This sermon was taken from *Memoirs of George Whitefield*, edited by John Gilles and published in 1837 by Hunt and Noyes. It can also be found in *Select Sermons of George Whitefield*, published by Banner of Truth Trust.

---— 1 ———

The Good Shepherd: A Farewell Sermon

My sheep hear my voice, and I know them, and they follow me:
and I give unto them eternal life; and they shall never perish,
neither shall any pluck them out of my hand. (John 10:27–28)

IT IS A COMMON AND, I BELIEVE, GENERALLY SPEAKING, my dear
hearers, a true saying, that bad manners beget good laws.
Whether this will hold good in every particular in respect to
the affairs of this world, I am persuaded the observation is very
pertinent in respect to the things of another. I mean bad
manners, bad treatment, bad words have been overruled by
the sovereign grace of God to produce and to be the cause of
the best sermons that were ever delivered from the mouth of
the God-man, Christ Jesus.

One would have imagined that as He came clothed with divine efficiency, as He came with divine credentials, as He spoke
as never man spoke, that no one would have been able to have
resisted the wisdom with which He spoke. One would imagine
they would have been so struck with the demonstration of the
Spirit that with one consent they would all own that He was
that prophet that was to be raised up "like unto Moses" (see
Deut. 34:10). But you seldom find our Lord preaching a sermon but something or other that He said was caviled at; no,

9

their enmity frequently broke through all good manners. They often, therefore, interrupted Him while He was preaching, which shows the enmity of their hearts, long before God permitted it to be in their power to shed His innocent blood. If we look no further than this chapter where He represents Himself as a Good Shepherd, one that laid down His life for His sheep, we see the best return He had was to be looked upon as possessed or distracted. We are told that there was a division therefore again among the Jews for these sayings, and many of them said, "He hath a devil and is mad; why hear ye him?" (John 10:20). If the Master of the house was served so, pray what are the servants to expect? Others, a little more sober minded, said, "These are not the words of him that hath a devil" (v. 21). The Devil never used to preach or act in this way. "Can a devil open the eyes of the blind?" (v. 21). So He had some friends among this rabble. This did not discourage our Lord. He goes on in His work. We shall never, never go on with the work of God until, like our Master, we are willing to go through good and through evil report. Let the Devil see we are not so complaisant as to stop one moment for his harking at us as we go along.

We are told that our Lord was at Jerusalem at the Feast of the Dedication, and it was winter. The Feast of Dedication held, I think, seven or eight days, was for the commemoration of the restoration of the temple and altar, after its profanation by Antiochus. Now this was certainly a mere human institution and had no divine image, no divine superscription upon it. Yet I do not find that our blessed Lord and Master preached against it. I do not find that He spent His time about this. His heart was too big with superior things. I believe when we, like Him, are filled with the Holy Spirit, we shall not entertain our audiences with disputes about rites and ceremonies but shall treat upon the essentials of the gospel, and then rites and ceremonies will appear with more indifference. Our Lord does not say that He would not go up to the feast. For on the contrary, He did go there, not so much to keep the feast as to have an opportunity to spread the gospel net, and that should be our method, not to follow disputing. It is the glory of the Methodists that we have been in existence forty years, and I thank God that there has not been one single pamphlet written by any of our preachers about the nonessentials of religion.

Our Lord always made the best of every opportunity; and we are told that He "walked in the temple in Solomon's porch" (v. 23). One would have thought the scribes and Pharisees would have put Him in one of their stalls and have complimented Him with desiring Him to preach. No, they let Him walk in Solomon's porch. Some think He walked by Himself, nobody choosing to keep company with Him. I see Him walking and looking at the temple and foreseeing within Himself how soon it would be destroyed. He walked pensive to see the dreadful calamities that would come upon the land, for not knowing the day of its visitation. It was to let the world see that he was not afraid to appear in public. He walked as much as to say, Have any of you anything to say to me? And He put Himself in their way, that if they had anything to ask Him, He was ready to resolve them. He wanted to show them that though they had treated Him so ill, yet He was ready to preach salvation to them.

In the twenty-fourth verse we are told, "Then came the Jews round about him, and said unto him, How long dost thou make us to doubt?" (v. 24). They came around Him when they saw Him walking in Solomon's porch. Now, they say, we will have Him; now we will attack Him. And now was fulfilled that passage in the Psalms, "They compassed me about like bees" (118:12) to sting me, or rather like wasps. Now, they say, we will get Him in the middle of us and see what sort of a man He is. We will see whether we cannot conquer Him. They came to Him and said, "How long dost thou make us to doubt?" Now this seems a plausible question: "How long dost thou make us to doubt?" Pray how long, Sir, do You intend to keep us in suspense? Some think the words will bear this interpretation: Pray, Sir, how long do You intend thus to steal away our hearts? They would represent Him to be a designing man like Absalom to get the people on

His side and then set up Himself for the Messiah. Thus, carnal minds always interpret good men's actions. But the meaning seems to be this, they were doubting concerning Christ. Doubting Christians may think it is God's fault that they doubt, but God knows it is all their own. "How long dost thou make us to doubt?"

I wish you would speak a little plainer, Sir, and not let us have any more of Your parables. Pray let us know who You are, let us have it from Your own mouth. "If thou be the Christ, tell us plainly" (v. 24). I do not doubt but they put on a very sanctified face and looked very demure. "If thou be the Christ, tell us plainly," intending to catch Him. If He does not say He is the Christ, we will say He is ashamed of His own cause. If He does tell us plainly that He is the Christ, then we will impeach Him to the governor. We will go and tell the governor that this man says He is the Messiah. Now we know of no Messiah but what is to jostle Caesar out of his throne. The Devil always wants to make it believed that God's people (who are the most loyal people in the world) are rebels to the government under which they live. "If thou be the Christ, tell us plainly."

Our Lord does not let them wait long for an answer. Honesty can soon speak: "I told you, and ye believed not: the works that I do in my Father's name, they bear witness of me" (v. 25). Had our Lord said, "I am the Messiah," they would have taken Him up. He knew that and, therefore, joined *the wisdom of the serpent* with *the innocence of the dove*. He says, "I appeal to My works and doctrine, and if you will not infer from them that I am the Messiah, I have no further argument." He adds, "But ye believe not, because ye are not of my sheep" (v. 26). He complains twice, for their unbelief was the greatest grief of heart to Christ. Then He goes on in the words of our text, "My sheep hear my voice, and I know them, and they follow me: and I give unto them eternal life; and they shall never perish, neither shall any pluck them out of my hand." "My sheep hear my voice." You think to puzzle, you think to chagrin Me with this kind of conduct, but you are mistaken. You do not believe on Me because you are not of My sheep. The great Mr. Stodart of New England (and no place under heaven produces greater divines than New England) preached once from these words, "But ye believe not, because ye are not of my sheep." A very strange text to preach upon to convince a congregation, yet God so blessed it that two or three hundred souls were awakened by that sermon. God grant such success to attend the labors of all His faithful ministers.

"My sheep hear my voice, and they follow me." It is very remarkable, there are but two sorts of people mentioned in Scripture. It does not say the Baptists and Independents, nor the Methodists and Presbyterians; no, Jesus Christ divides the whole world into but two classes—sheep and goats. The Lord give us to see this morning to which of these classes we belong.

But it is observable, believers are always compared to something that is good and profitable, and unbelievers are always described by something that is bad, and good for little or nothing.

If you ask me why Christ's people are called sheep, as God shall enable me I will give you a short answer, and I hope it will be to you an answer of peace. Sheep, you know, generally love to be together. We say a flock of sheep not a herd of sheep. Sheep are little creatures. Christ's people may be called sheep because they are little in the eyes of the world, and they are yet less in their own eyes. O some people think if the great men were on our side, if we had king, lords, and commons on our side—I mean if they were all true believers—O if we had all the kings upon the earth on our side! Suppose you had? Alas! alas! do you think the church would go on the better? Why, if it was fashionable to be a Methodist at court, if it was fashionable to be a Methodist abroad, they would go with a Bible or a hymnbook instead of a novel. But religion never thrives under too much sunshine. "Not many mighty, not many noble, are called: but God hath chosen the foolish things of the world to confound the wise; and God hath chosen the weak things of the world to confound the things which are mighty" (1 Cor.

1:26–27). Dr. Watts says, "Here and there I see a king, and here and there a great man in heaven, but their number is but small."

Sheep are looked upon to be the most harmless and quiet creatures that God has made. O may God of His infinite mercy give us to know that we are His sheep by our having this blessed temper infused into our hearts by the Holy Spirit. "Learn of me," says our blessed Lord. To do what? To work miracles? No. "Learn of me; for I am meek and lowly in heart" (Matt. 11:29). A very good man now living said once, "If there is any one particular temper I desire more than another, it is the grace of *meekness*, quietly to bear bad treatment, to forget and forgive; and at the same time that I am sensible I am injured, not to be overcome of evil, but to have grace given me to overcome evil with good." To the honor of Moses, it is declared that he was the meekest man upon earth. Meekness is necessary for people in power. A man that is passionate is dangerous. Every governor should have a warm temper, but a man of an unrelenting, unforgiving temper is no more fit for government than Phaeton to drive the chariot of the sun. He only sets the world on fire.

You all know that sheep, of all the creatures in the world, are the most apt to stray and be lost. Christ's people may justly, in that respect, be compared to sheep. Therefore, in the introduction to our morning service, we say, "We have erred and strayed from thy ways like lost sheep." Turn out a horse or a dog and they will find the way home, but a sheep wanders about bleating here and there as much as to say, "Dear stranger, show me my home again." Thus, Christ's sheep are too apt to wander from the fold. Having their eye off the Great Shepherd, they go into this field and that field, over this hedge and that, and often return home with the loss of their wool.

But at the same time, sheep are the most useful creatures in the world. They manure the land and, thereby, prepare it for the seed. They clothe our bodies with wool, and there is not the least part of a sheep but is useful to man. O my friends, God grant that you and I may, in this respect, answer the character of sheep. The world says because we preach faith we deny good works. This is the usual objection against the doctrine of imputed righteousness, but it is slander, an imputed slander. It was a maxim in the time of the first reformers, that though the Arminians preached up good works, you must go to the Calvinists for them. Christ's sheep study to be useful and to clothe all they can. We should labor with our hands that we may have to give to all those that need.

Believers consider Christ's property in them; He says, *"My sheep."* O blessed be God for that little, dear, great word *my*. We are His by eternal election: "The sheep which thou hast given me," says Christ (see John 17:9). They were given by God the Father to Christ Jesus in the covenant made between the Father and the Son from all eternity. They that are not led to see this, I wish them better heads; though I believe numbers that are against it have better hearts. The Lord help us to bear with one another where there is an honest heart.

He calls them *"my sheep."* They are His by purchase. O sinner, sinner, you have come this morning to hear a poor creature take *his last farewell*. But I want you to forget the creature that is preaching. I want to lead you farther than the tabernacle. Where do you want to lead us? Why, to Mount Calvary, there to see at what expense of blood Christ purchased those whom He calls His own. He redeemed them with His own blood, so that they are not only His by eternal election but also by actual redemption in time. They were given to Him by the Father upon the condition that He should redeem them by His heart's blood. It was a hard bargain, but Christ was willing to strike the bargain that you and I might not be damned forever.

They are His because they are enabled in a day of God's power voluntarily to give themselves up to Him. Christ says of these sheep especially that *they hear his voice, and that they follow him.* Will you be so good as to mind that? Here is an allusion to a shepherd. In some places in Scripture the shepherd is represented as going after the sheep (2 Sam. 7:8; Ps. 78:71). That is our way in England. But in the eastern nations the shepherds

generally went before. They held up their crook, and they had
a particular call that the sheep understood. Now says Christ,
"My sheep hear my voice." "This is my beloved Son," says God,
"hear him" (Mark. 9:7; Luke 9:35). And again, "The dead shall
hear the voice of the Son of God: and . . . live" (John 5:25).
Now the question is, what do we understand by hearing Christ's
voice?

First, we hear Moses' voice. We hear the voice of the Law.
There is no going to Mount Zion but by the way of Mount Sinai;
that is the right straight road. I know some say they do not
know when they were converted. Those are, I believe, very few.
Generally, I may say almost always, God deals otherwise. Some
are, indeed, called sooner by the Lord than others. But before
they are made to see the glory of God, they must hear the voice
of the Law. So you must hear the voice of the Law before you
will ever be savingly called to God. You never throw off your
cloak in a storm but hug it the closer, so the Law makes a man
hug close his corruptions (Rom. 8:7–9). But when the gospel
of the Son of God shines into their souls, then they throw off
the corruptions that they have hugged so closely. They hear
His voice saying, "Son, daughter, be of good cheer, thy sins,
which are many, are all forgiven thee" (see Matt. 9:2; Luke 7:47).
They hear his voice, that bespeaks the habitual temper of their
minds. The wicked hear the voice of the Devil, the lusts of the
flesh, the lusts of the eye, and the pride of life. Christ's sheep
themselves attended to them before conversion. But when
called afterward by God, they hear the voice of a Redeemer's
blood speaking peace to them—they hear the voice of His word
and of His Spirit.

The consequence of hearing His voice and the proof that
we do hear His voice will be to follow Him. Jesus said to His
disciples, "If any man will come after me, let him deny himself, and take up his cross, and follow me" (Matt. 16:24; see
Mark 8:34; Luke 9:23). And it is said of the saints in glory that
they followed the Lamb whithersoever he went (see Rev. 14:4). Wherever the shepherd turns his crook, and the sheep hear his voice,

they follow him. They often tread one upon another and hurt one another because they are in such haste on their way to heaven. Following Christ means following Him through life—following Him in every word and gesture—following Him out of one clime into another. "Bid me come unto thee on the water," said Peter (Matt. 14:28). And if we are commanded to go over the water for Christ, God, if His infinite mercy, follow us! We must first be sure that the Great Shepherd points His crook for us. But this is the character of a true servant of Christ, that He endeavors to follow Christ in thought, word, and work.

Now, my friends, before we go farther, as this is the last opportunity I shall have of speaking to you for some months if we live (some of you I suppose, do not choose in general to rise so soon as you have this morning; now I hope the world did not get into your hearts before you left your beds), now you are here, do let me entreat you to inquire whether you belong to Christ's sheep or not. Man, woman, sinner, put your hand to your heart and answer me, Did you ever hear Christ's voice so as to follow Him, to give up yourself without reserve to Him? I verily do believe from my inmost soul—and that is my comfort now that I am about to take my leave of you—that I am preaching to a vast body, a multitude of dear, precious souls who, if it was proper for you to speak, would say thanks be to God that we can follow Jesus in the character of sheep, though we are ashamed to think how often we wander from You and what little fruit we bring to You. If that is the language of your hearts, I wish you joy. Welcome, welcome, dear soul, to Christ. O blessed be God for His rich grace, His distinguishing, sovereign, electing love, by which He has distinguished you and me. And if He has been pleased to let you hear His voice through the ministration of a poor, miserable sinner—a poor, but happy pilgrim—may the Lord Jesus Christ have all the glory

If you belong to Jesus Christ, He is speaking of you, for He says, *I know my sheep.* I know them. What does that mean? Why, He knows their number, He knows their names, He knows

everyone for whom He died. If there was to be one missing
for whom Christ died, God the Father would send Him down
again from heaven to fetch him. He says, "Of them which thou
gavest me, have I lost none" (John 18:9). Christ knows His
sheep. He not only knows their number, but the words speak
the peculiar knowledge and notice He takes of them. He takes
as much care of them as if there was but one single sheep in
the world. To the hypocrite he says, "Verily . . . I know you
not" (Matt. 25:12). But He knows His saints. He is acquainted
with all their sorrows, trials, and temptations. He bottles up all
their tears. He knows their inward corruptions, and all their
wanderings, and He takes care to fetch them back again. I remember I heard good Dr. Marryant, who was a good market-
language preacher, once say at Pinner's Hall (I hope that pulpit
will always be filled with such preachers), "God has got a great
dog to fetch his sheep back." Do you not know that when the
sheep wander, the shepherd sends his dog after them to fetch
them back again? So when Christ's sheep wander, He lets the
Devil go after them and suffers him to bark at them, who, instead of driving them farther off, is made a means to bring
them back again to Christ's fold.

There is a precious word I would have you take notice of, "I
know them," that may comfort you under all your trials. We
sometimes think that Christ does not hear our prayers, that
He does not know us. We are ready to suspect that He has
forgotten to be gracious, but what a mercy it is that He does
know us. We accuse one another, turn devils to one another,
are accusers of the brethren. What will support two of God's
people when judged by one another, but this, "Lord, You know
my integrity; You know how matters are with me!"

But, my friends, here is something better, here is good news
for you. What is that? Why, "I give unto them eternal life; and
they shall never perish, neither shall any pluck them out of my hand."
O that the words may come to your hearts with as much warmth
and power as they did to mine thirty-five years ago. I never
prayed against any corruption I had in my life so much as I

did against going into holy orders, so soon as my friends were for having me go. Bishop Benson was pleased to honor me with peculiar friendship, so as to offer me preferment or do anything for me. My friends wanted me to mount the church speedily. They wanted me to knock my head against the pulpit too young. How some young men stand up here and there and preach, I do not know. But God knows how deep a concern entering into the ministry and preaching was to me. I have prayed a thousand times until the sweat has dropped from my face like rain that God of His infinite mercy would not let me enter the church before He called me to and thrust me forth in His work.

I remember once in Gloucester (I know the room. I look up at the window when I am there and walk along the streets. I know the window, the bedside, and the floor upon which I have lain prostrate) that I said, Lord, I cannot go. I shall be puffed up with pride and fall into the condemnation of the Devil. Lord, do not let me go yet. I pleaded to be at Oxford two or three years more. I intended to make a hundred and fifty sermons, and thought I would set up with a good stock in trade. But I remember praying, wrestling, and striving with God. I said I am undone, I am unfit to preach in Your great name. Send me not, pray, Lord, send me not yet. I wrote to all my friends in town and country to pray against the bishop's solicitation, but they insisted I should go into orders before I was twenty-two. After all their solicitation these words came into my mind: *Nothing shall pluck you out of My hand.* O may the words be blessed to you, my dear friends, that I am parting with as they were to me when they came warm upon my heart. Then, and not until then, did I say, Lord, I will go, send me when You will.

I remember when I was in a place called Dover Island near Georgia, we put in with bad winds. I had a hundred and fifty in the family to maintain and not a single farthing to do it with in the dearest part of the king's dominions. I remember I told a minister of Christ now in heaven, "I had these words once, sir: *Nothing shall pluck you out of My hand.*" "O," says he, "take comfort from them: you may be sure God will be as good as His word, if He never tells you so again." And our Lord knew His poor sheep would be always doubting they should never reach heaven, therefore, says He, "I give unto them eternal life, and they shall never perish."

Here in our text are three blessed declarations, and promises: *First, "I know them."*

Second, "They shall never perish." Though they often think they shall perish by the hand of their lusts and corruptions, though they think they shall perish by the deceitfulness of their hearts, but Christ says, *"They shall never perish."* I have brought them out of the world to myself, and do you think I will let them go to hell after that? *"I give unto them eternal life."* Pray mind that, not I will, but I do. Some talk of being justified at the day of judgment. That is nonsense. If we are not justified here, we shall not be justified there. He gives them eternal life, that is, the earnest, the pledge, and assurance of it. The indwelling of the Spirit of God here is the earnest of glory hereafter.

Third, "Neither shall any pluck them out of my hand." He holds them in His hand, that is, He holds them by His power, none shall pluck them from there. There is always something plucking at Christ's sheep, the Devil, the lusts of the flesh, the lusts of the eye, and the pride of life, all try to pluck them out of Christ's hand. O my friends, they need not pluck us, for we help all three to pluck ourselves out of the hand of Jesus. "But none shall pluck them out of My hand," says Christ. "I give to them eternal life. I am going to heaven to prepare a place for them, and there they shall be" (see John 14:3). O my friends, if it was not for keeping you too long and too much exhausting my own spirits, I could call upon you to leap for joy. There is not a more blessed text to support the final perseverance of the saints. I am astonished any poor soul, and good people I hope too, can fight against the doctrine of the perseverance of the saints. What if a person says they should persevere in wickedness? Ah, that is an abuse of the doctrine. What, because some people spoil good food, are we never to eat it? But, my friends, upon this text I can leave my cares, all my friends, all Christ's sheep to the protection of Christ Jesus' never failing love.

I thought this morning when I came here riding from the other end of the town, it was to me like coming to be executed publicly. When the carriage turned just at the end of the walk and I saw you running here, O I thought, it is like a person now coming to the place where he is to be executed. When I went up to put on my gown, I thought it was like dressing myself to be made a public spectacle to shed my blood for Christ. I take all heaven and earth to witness, and God and the holy angels to witness, that though I had preferment enough offered me, that though the bishop took me in his arms and offered me two parishes when I was but twenty-two years old and always took me to his table, though I had preferment enough offered me when I was ordained, You, O God, know that when the bishop put his hand upon my head, I looked for no other preferment than publicly to suffer for the Lamb of God. In this spirit I came out, in this spirit I came up to this metropolis.

I was thinking when I read of Jacob's going over the brook with a staff that I would not say so much, but I came up without a friend. I went to Oxford without a friend. I had not a servant. I had no one to introduce me. But God, by His Holy Spirit, was pleased to raise me up to preach for His great name's sake. Through His divine Spirit I continue to this day and feel my affections are as strong as ever toward the work and the people of the living God. The congregations at both ends of the town are dear to me. God has honored me to build this and the other place. Blessed be His name, as He called me to Georgia at first, and I left all London affairs to God's care when I had most of the churches in London open for me and had twelve or fourteen constables to keep the doors that people might not crowd too much. I had offers of hundreds then to settle in London. Yet I gave it up for God to go into a foreign clime, and I hope with that same single intention I am going now.

When I came from America last, I thought I had no other

river to pass over but the river Jordan. I remember I told you so. As the orphan house was then to be given, I thought, out of my hands, I intended to retire into some little corner and pray when I could not preach, my spirits were so low and my nerves and animal frame so weak, but God in His infinite mercy has renewed my strength and is pleased to raise my spirits so that I find my heart is willing to go here or there wherever God shall call.

The orphan house being turned into a college is a matter of great consequence. You that have not been in America cannot tell, but I heartily wish (I am neither a prophet, nor the son of a prophet) and I hope none of us will ever be driven to America for an asylum, where God's people were driven from this land a hundred years ago. Clouds are growing thick, and if a spirit of moderation does not prevail among governors and governed, what but confusion must happen to persons who strive with one another and are making sport for the Devil by destroying one another? May the great and gracious God avert every impending storm. By diffusing a spirit of moderation and of a sound mind, and by keeping His people close to Himself, may God avert those storms, those terrible judgments, that we have reason to expect from our repeated provocations. I am going now to settle the orphan house upon a proper basis. I go now in the fall, that I may be in Georgia in the winter, which is fine weather there. The twenty-fifth of March is the anniversary of the day on which I laid the first brick of the orphan house. By that time I hope all the buildings will be finished and the plantation settled. Then I hope to go and preach along the continent to New England, and from there I intend, if God permit me, to return to my dear London and English friends again.

I have blessed news from the orphan house. One writes to me word, "Would to God you could send a thousand such as you have sent Mr. Dixon and his wife, who have been old servants there, Mr. Wright, Mr. Crayne, and Mr. Wright's brother, and those that have been employed with them to carry on the work of the Lord." I cannot think but God intends to lay a foundation for a blessed seminary for Christ. Lord Jesus, hear our prayers upon that account.

Now I must come to the hardest part I have to act. I was afraid when I came out from home that I could not bear the shock, but I hope the Lord Jesus Christ will help me to bear it and help you to give me up to the blessed God, let Him do with me what He will. This is the thirteenth time of my crossing the mighty waters. It is a little difficult at this time of life. Though my spirits are improved in some degree, yet weakness is the best of my strength. But I delight in the cause, and God fills me with a peace that is unutterable, which nobody knows and a stranger intermeddles not with. Into His hands I commend my spirit, and I beg that this may be the language of your hearts, "Lord keep him, let nothing pluck him out of Your hands." I expect many a trial while I am on board. Satan always meets me there. But that God who has kept me, I believe will keep me. I thank God I have the honor of leaving everything quite well and easy at both ends of the town. My dear hearers, my prayers to God shall be that nothing shall pluck you out of Christ's hands. Witness against me, if I ever set up a party for myself. Did ever any minister, or could any minister in the world say that I ever spoke against anyone going to any dear minister? I thank God that He has enabled me to be always strengthening the hands of all, though some have afterward been ashamed to own me. I declare to you that I believe that God will be with me and will strengthen me. I believe it is in answer to your prayers that God is pleased to revive my spirits; may the Lord help you to pray on. If I am drowned in the waves, I will say, "Lord, take care of my London, take care of my English friends, let nothing pluck them out of Your hands."

And as Christ has given us eternal life, O my friends, some of you, I doubt not, will be gone to Him before my return. But my dear friends, my dear hearers, never mind that; we shall part, but it will be to meet again forever. I dare not meet you now, I cannot bear your coming to me to part from me, it cuts me to the heart and quite overcomes me. But by and by all

parting will be over and all tears shall he wiped away from our
eyes. God grant that none that weep now at my parting may
weep at our meeting at the day of judgment. If you never were
among Christ's sheep before, may Christ Jesus bring you now.
O come, come, see what it is to have eternal life. Do not refuse
it. Haste sinner, haste away; may the great, the Good Shepherd
draw your souls. O! if you never heard His voice before, God
grant you may hear it now that I may have this comfort when I
am gone that I had last, that some souls were awakened at the
parting sermon. O that it may be a farewell sermon to you, that
it may be a means of your taking a farewell of the world, the
lusts of the flesh, the lusts of the eye, and the pride of life. O
come, come, come to the Lord Jesus Christ—to Him I leave you.

And you, dear sheep, that are already in His hands, O may
God keep you from wandering. May God keep you near Christ's
feet. I do not care what shepherds keep you, so as you are kept
near the Great Shepherd and Bishop of our souls (see 1 Peter
2:25). The Lord God keep you, lift up the light of His counte-
nance upon you, and give you peace. Amen.

NOTES

The Good Shepherd

Frederick W. Robertson (1816–1853) wanted to be a soldier, but he yielded to his father's decision that he take orders in the Anglican church. The courage that he would have shown on the battlefield, he displayed in the pulpit, where he fearlessly declared truth as he saw it. Never strong physically, he experienced deep depression; he questioned his faith, and he often wondered if his ministry was doing any good. He died a young man, in great pain, but in great faith and courage as well. He had ministered for only six years at Trinity Chapel, Brighton, but today his printed sermons have taken his brave message around the world.

This sermon was taken from his *Sermons, Second Series,* published in 1900 in London by Kegan Paul, Trench, Trubner and Company.

2

The Good Shepherd

I am the good shepherd, and know my sheep, and am known of mine. As the Father knoweth me, even so know I the Father: and I lay down my life for the sheep. (John 10:14–15)

As these words stand in the English translation, it is hard to see any connection between the thoughts that are brought together.

It is asserted that Christ is the Good Shepherd and knows His sheep. It is also asserted that He knows the Father, but between these two truths there is no express connection. And again, it is declared that He lays down His life for the sheep. This follows directly after the assertion that He knows the Father. Again, we are at a loss to say what one of these truths has to do with the other.

But the whole difficulty vanishes with the alteration of a single stop and a single word. Let the words *even so* be exchanged for the word *and*. Four times in these verses the same word occurs. Three times out of these four it is translated "and"—*and* know my sheep, *and* am known, *and* I lay down my life. All that is required then is, that in consistency it shall be translated by the same word in the fourth case: for *even so* substitute *and*. Then strike away the full stop after *mine* and read the whole sentence thus: "I am the good shepherd, and know my sheep, and am known of mine as the Father knoweth me, *and* as I know the Father: and I lay down my life for the sheep."

At once our Redeemer's thought becomes clear. There is a reciprocal affection between the Shepherd and the sheep. There is a reciprocal affection between the Father and the Son; the one is the parallel of the other. The affection between the divine Shepherd and His flock can be compared, for the closeness of its intimacy, with nothing but the affection between the eternal Father and the Son of His love. As the Father knows the Son, so does the Shepherd know the sheep; as the Son knows the Father, so do the sheep know their heavenly Shepherd.

The Pastoral Character Claimed by Christ

The Son of Man claims to Himself the name of Shepherd. Now we shall not learn anything from that, unless we enter humbly and affectionately into the spirit of Christ's teaching. It is the heart alone that can give us a key to His words. Recollect *how* He taught. By metaphors, by images, by illustrations, boldly figurative, in rich variety—yes, in daring abundance. He calls Himself a gate, a king, a vine, a shepherd, a thief in the night. In every one of these He appeals to certain feelings and associations. What He says can only be interpreted by such associations. They must be understood by a living heart; a cold, clear intellect will make nothing of them. If you take those glorious expressions, pregnant with almost boundless thought, and lay them down as so many articles of rigid, stiff theology, you turn life into death. It is just as if a chemist were to analyze a fruit or a flower, and then imagine that he had told you what a fruit and a flower are. He separates them into their elements, names them, and numbers them. But those elements, weighed, measured, numbered in the exact proportions that made up the beautiful living thing are not the living thing—no, nor anything like it. Your science is very profound, no doubt; but the fruit is crushed, and the grace of the flower is gone.

It is in this way often that we deal with the words of Christ, when we anatomize them and analyze them. Theology is very necessary, chemistry is very necessary. But chemistry destroys life to analyze, murders to dissect; theology very often kills religion out of words before it can cut them up into propositions.

Here is a living truth that our cold reasonings have often torn into dead fragments—"I am the good Shepherd." In this northern England, it is hard to get the living associations of the East with which such an expression is full.

The pastoral life and duty in the East is very unlike that of the shepherds on our bleak hillsides and downs. Here the connection between the shepherd and the sheep is simply one of pecuniary interest. Ask an English shepherd about his flock, he can tell you the numbers and the value. He knows the market in which each was purchased, and the remunerating price at which it can he disposed of. There is before him so much stock convertible into so much money.

Beneath the burning skies and the clear starry nights of Palestine there grows up between the shepherd and his flock a union of attachment and tenderness. It is the country where at any moment sheep are liable to be swept away by some mountain torrent, or carried off by hill robbers, or torn by wolves. At any moment their protector may have to save them by personal hazard. The shepherd king tells us how in defense of his father's flock he slew a lion and a bear, and Jacob reminds Laban how he watched Laban's sheep in the day the drought consumed. Every hour of the shepherd's life is risk. Sometimes for the sake of an armful of grass in the parched summer days, he must climb precipices almost perpendicular and stand on a narrow ledge of rock where the wild goat will scarcely venture. Pitiless showers, driving snows, long hours of thirst—all this he must endure if the flock is to be kept at all.

And, thus, there grows up between the man and the dumb creatures he protects a kind of friendship. For this is after all the true school in which love is taught, dangers mutually shared, and hardships borne together. These are the things that make generous friendship—risk cheerfully encountered for another's

sake. You love those for whom you risk, and they love you.
Therefore, it is that, not as here where the flock is driven, the
shepherd goes before and the sheep follow him. They follow
in perfect trust, even though he should be leading them away
from a green pasture, by a rocky road, to another pasture that
they cannot yet see. He knows them all—their separate histo-
ries, their ailments, their characters.

Now let it be observed, how much in all this connection there
is of *heart*—of real, personal attachment, almost inconceivable
to us. It is strange how deep the sympathy may become between the higher and the lower being, even between the being
that has life and what is lifeless. Alone almost in the desert,
the Arab and his horse are one family. Alone in those vast soli-
tudes, with no human being near, the shepherd and the sheep
feel a life in common. Differences disappear, the vast interval
between the man and the brute, the single point of union is
felt strongly. One is the love of the protector; the other the
love of the grateful life. So between lives so distant there is
woven by night and day, by summer suns and winter frosts a
living network of sympathy. The greater and the less mingle
their being together; they feel each other. The shepherd knows
his sheep, and is known of them.

The men to whom Christ said these words felt all this and
more the moment He had said them that which it has taken me
many minutes to draw out in dull sentences. For He appealed
to the familiar associations of their daily life, and calling Himself a Shepherd, touched strings which would vibrate with many
a tender and pure recollection of their childhood. And unless
we try by realizing such scenes to supply what they felt by association, the words of Christ will be only hard, dry, lifeless words
to us. For all Christ's teaching is a divine poetry, luxuriant in
metaphor, overflowing with truth too large for accurate sentences, truth which only a heart alive can appreciate. More than
half the heresies into which Christian sects have blundered have
merely come from mistaking for dull prose what prophets and
apostles said in those highest moments of the soul, when sera-

phim kindle the sentences of the pen and lip into poetry. "This is my body" (Matt. 26:26; Mark 14:22; Luke 22:19; 1 Cor. 11:24). Chill that into prose, and it becomes transubstantiation. "I am the good shepherd." In the dry and merciless logic of a commentary, trying laboriously to find out minute points of ingenious resemblance in which Christ is like a shepherd, the glory and the tenderness of this sentence are dried up.

But try to feel by imagining what the lonely Syrian shepherd must feel toward the helpless things that are the companions of his daily life. For their safety he stands in jeopardy every hour, and their value is measurable to him not by price but by his own jeopardy. Then we have reached some notion of the love that Jesus meant to represent, that eternal tenderness that bends over us—infinitely lower though we be in nature—and knows the name of each and the trials of each, and thinks for each with a separate solicitude, and gave itself for each with a sacrifice as special and a love as personal, as if in the whole world's wilderness there were none other but that one.

To the name *shepherd,* Christ adds an emphatic word of much significance: "I am the *good* shepherd." Good, not in the sense of benevolent, but in the sense of genuine, true born, of the real kind—just as wine of nobler quality is good compared with the cheaper sort, just as a soldier is good or noble who is a soldier in heart and not a soldier by mere profession or for pay. It is the same word used by St. Paul when he speaks of a good soldier, that is, a noble soldier of Christ. Certain peculiar qualifications make the genuine soldier—certain peculiar qualifications make the genuine or good shepherd.

Now this expression distinguishes the shepherd from two sorts of men who may also be keepers of the sheep—shepherds, but not shepherds of the true blood. First, there are the robbers. Second, there are the hirelings.

Robbers may turn shepherds. They may keep the sheep, but they guard them only for their own purposes, simply for the flesh and fleece. They have not a true shepherd's heart, any more than a pirate has the true sailor's heart and the true sailor's loyalty. There were many such marauders on the hills of Galilee and Judea. Such, for example, as those from whom David and his band protected Nabal's flocks on Mount Carmel.

And many such nominal shepherds had the people of Israel had in bygone years: rulers in whom the art of ruling had been but kingcraft, and teachers whose instruction to the people had been but priestcraft. Government, statesmanship, teachership—these are pastoral callings—sublime, even godlike. For only consider it—wise rule, chivalrous protection, loving guidance—what diviner work than these has the Master given to the shepherds of the people? But when the work is done, even well done, whether it be by statesmen or by pastors, for the sake of party, or place, or honor, or personal consistency, or preferment, it is not the spirit of the genuine shepherd but of the robber. No wonder He said, "All that ever came before me are thieves and robbers" (John 10:8).

Again, *hirelings are shepherds,* but not good shepherds of the right pure kind. They are tested by danger. "He that is an hireling, and not the shepherd, whose own the sheep are not, seeth the wolf coming, and leaveth the sheep, and fleeth: and the wolf catcheth them, and scattereth the sheep" (v. 12). Now a man is a hireling when he does his duty for pay. He may do it in his way faithfully. The paid shepherd would not desert the sheep for a shower or a cold night. But the lion and the bear—he is not paid to risk his life against them, and the sheep are not his, so he leaves them to their fate. So, in the same way, a man may be a hired priest, as Demetrius was at Ephesus: "By this craft we get our living." Or he may be a paid demagogue, a great champion of rights and an investigator of abuses, paid by applause. While popularity lasts, he will be a reformer—deserting the people when danger comes. There is no vital union between the champion and the defenseless—the teacher and the taught. The cause of the sheep is not *his* cause.

Exactly the reverse of this Christ asserts in calling Himself the *Good* Shepherd. He is a good, genuine, or true-born sailor who feels that the ship is as it were His own; whose point of chivalrous honor is to save His ship rather than Himself—not to survive her. He is a good, genuine, or true-born shepherd who has the spirit of His calling, is an enthusiast in it, has the true shepherd's heart, and makes the cause of the sheep His cause.

The cause of man was the cause of Christ! He did no hireling's work. The only pay He got was hatred, a crown of thorns, and the cross. He might have escaped it all. He might have been the Leader of the people and their King. He might have converted the idolatry of an hour into the hosannas of a lifetime, if He would have but conciliated the Pharisees instead of bidding them defiance and exasperating their bigotry against Him; if He would have but explained, and, like some demagogue called to account, trimmed away His sublime sharp-edged truths about oppression and injustice until they became harmless, because meaningless; if He would have but left unsaid those rough things about the consecrated temple and the Sabbath days; if He would have but left undisputed the hereditary title of Israel to God's favor and not stung the national vanity by telling them that trust in God justifies the Gentile as entirely as the Jew; if He would have but taught less prominently that hateful doctrine of the salvability of the heathen Gentiles and the heretic Samaritans and the universal Fatherhood of God; if He would have but stated with less angularity of edge His central truth—that not by mere compliance with law, but by a spirit transcending law, even the spirit of the cross and self-sacrifice, can the soul of man be atoned to God—that would have saved Him. But that would have been the desertion of the cause—God's cause and man's—the cause of the ignorant defenseless sheep, whose very salvation depended on the keeping of that gospel intact. Therefore the Shepherd gave His life as a witness to the truth and as a sacrifice to God. It was a profound truth that the populace gave utterance to when they taunted Him on the cross, "He saved others; himself he cannot save" (Matt. 27:42; Mark 15:31). No, of course not; He that will save others *cannot* save Himself.

The Proofs That Substantiate the Claim

Of that pastoral character, He gives here three proofs: (1) "I . . . know my sheep," (2) "I . . . am known of mine," and (3) "I lay down my life for the sheep."

"*I . . . know my sheep. . . .* As the Father knoweth me." In other words, as unerringly as His Father read His heart, so unerringly did He read the heart of man and recognize His own.

We ask how? An easy reply, and a common one, would be that He recognized them by the Godhead in Him. His mind was divine, therefore omniscient. He knew all things; therefore, He knew what was in man, and He knew His own. But we must not slur over His precious words in this way. That divinity of His is made the passkey by which we open all mysteries with fatal facility and save ourselves from thinking of them. We get a dogma and cover truth with it. We satisfy ourselves with saying Christ was God and lose the precious humanities of His heart and life.

There is here a deep truth of human nature, for He does not limit that recognizing power to Himself. He says that the sheep know Him as truly as He the sheep. He knew men on the same principle as we know men—the same on which we know Him. The only difference is in degree. He knows with infinitely more unerringness than we, but the knowledge is the same in kind.

Let us think of this. There is a certain mysterious tact of sympathy and antipathy by which we discover the like and unlike of ourselves in other people's character. You cannot find out a man's opinions unless he chooses to express them; but his feelings and his character you may. He cannot hide them. You feel them in his look and mien, and tones and motion. There is, for instance, a certain something in sincerity and reality that cannot be mistaken—a certain something in real grief that the most artistic counterfeit cannot imitate. It is distinguished by nature not education. There is something in an impure heart that purity detects afar off. Marvelous it is how innocence perceives the approach of evil which it cannot know by experience,

just as the dove which has never seen a falcon trembles by instinct at its approach, just as a blind man detects by finer sen-
sitiveness the passing of the cloud which he cannot see
overshadowing the sun. It is wondrous how the truer we become, the more unerringly we know the *ring* of truth, discern
whether a man be true or not, and can fasten at once upon
the rising lie in word and look and dissembling act. Wondrous
how the charity of Christ in the heart finely perceives the slightest aberration from charity in others, in ungentle thought or
slanderous tone.

Therefore Christ knew His sheep, by that mystic power always finest in the best natures, most developed in the highest,
by which like detects what is like and what unlike itself. He was
perfect love, perfect truth, perfect purity; therefore He knew
what was in man and felt, as by another sense, afar off the shadows of unlovingness and falseness and impurity.

No one can have read the Gospels without remarking that
they ascribe to Him unerring skill in reading man. People, we
read, began to show enthusiasm for Him. But Jesus did not
trust Himself to them, "for he knew what was in man" (John
2:25). He knew that the flatterers of today would be the accusers of tomorrow. Nathaniel stood before Him. He had scarcely
spoken a word; but at once unhesitatingly, to Nathaniel's own
astonishment, "Behold an Israelite indeed, in whom is no guile!"
(1:47). There came to Him a young man with vast possessions;
a single sentence, an exaggerated epithet, an excited manner,
revealed his character. Enthusiastic and amiable, Jesus loved
him. He was capable of obedience, in life's sunshine and prosperity, and capable of aspiration after something more than
mere obedience, but not of sacrifice. Jesus tested him to the
quick, and the young man failed. He did not try to call him
back, for He knew what was in him and what was not. He read
through Zaccheus when he climbed into the sycamore tree,
despised by the people as a publican, really a son of Abraham;
through Judas, with his benevolent saying about the selling of
the alabaster box for the poor and his false kiss; through the

curses of the thief upon the cross, a faith that could be saved; through the zeal of the man who in a fit of enthusiasm offered to go with Him whithersoever He would. He read through the Pharisees, and His whole being shuddered with the recoil of utter and irreconcilable aversion.

It was as if His bosom was some mysterious mirror on which all that came near Him left a sullied or unsullied surface, detecting themselves by every breath.

Now distinguish that divine power from that cunning sagacity which men call knowingness in the matter of character. The worldly wise have maxims and rules, but the finer shades and delicacies of truth of character escape them. They would prudently avoid Zaccheus—a publican.

There is a very solemn aspect in which this power of Jesus to know man presents itself. It is this that qualifies Him for judgment—this perfection of human sympathy. Perfect sympathy with every most delicate line of good implies exquisite antipathy to every shadow of a shade of evil. God has given Him authority to execute judgment, also, because He is the Son of Man. On sympathy the final awards of heaven and hell are built—attraction and repulsion, the law of the magnet. To each pole all that has affinity with itself—*to* Christ all that is Christlike, *from* Christ all that is not Christlike—forever and forever. Eternal judgment is nothing more than the carrying out of these words, "I . . . know my sheep." For the obverse of them is, "I never knew *you:* depart from me, ye that work iniquity" (Matt. 7:23).

The second proof that Christ alleges of the genuineness of His pastorate is that His sheep know Him—*"I . . . am known of mine."*

How shall we recognize truth divine? What is the test by which we shall know whether it comes from God or not? They tell us we know Christ to be from God because He wrought miracles. We know a doctrine to be from God because we find it written, or because it is sustained by a universal consent of fathers.

That is—for observe what this argument implies—there is

something more evident than truth. Truth cannot prove itself; we want something else to prove it. Our souls judge of truth; our senses judge of miracles. The evidence of our senses—the lowest part of our nature—is more certain than the evidence of our souls, by which we must partake of God.

Now to say so is to say that you cannot be sure that it is midday or morning sunshine unless you look at the sundial. You cannot be sure that the sun is shining in the heavens unless you see its shadow on the dial plate. The dial is valuable to a man who never reads the heavens; the shadow is good for him who has not watched the sun. But for a man who lives in perpetual contemplation of the sun in heaven, the sunshine needs no evidence, and every hour is known.

Now Christ says, "My sheep know *Me.*" Wisdom is justified by her children. Not by some lengthened investigation, whether the shepherd's dress be the identical dress, and the staff and the crosier genuine, do the sheep recognize the shepherd. They know *Him* and hear His voice; they know Him as a man knows his friend.

They know Him, in short, *instinctively.* Just so does the soul recognize what is of God and true. Truth is like light visible in itself, not distinguished by the shadows that it casts. There is something in our souls of God, which corresponds with what is of God outside us and recognizes it by direct intuition—something in the true soul which corresponds with truth and knows it to be truth. Christ came with truth, and the true recognize it as true. The sheep know the shepherd, wanting no further evidence. Take a few examples: "God is love" (1 John 4:8, 16). "What shall a man give in exchange for his soul?" (Matt. 16:26; Mark 8:37). "He that findeth his life shall lose it: and he that loseth his life for my sake shall find it" (Matt. 10:39). "All things are possible to him that believeth" (Mark 9:23). "The sabbath was made for man, and not man for the sabbath" (2:27). "God is a Spirit" (John 4:24).

Now the wise men of intellect and logical acumen wanted proof of these truths. Give us, said they, your credentials. "By what authority doest thou these things?" (Matt. 21:23; Mark 11:28; Luke 20:2). They wanted a sign from heaven to prove that the truth was true, and the life He led godlike, and not devil-like. How can we be sure that it is not from Beelzebub, the prince of the devils, that these deeds and sayings come? We must be quite sure that we are not taking a message from hell as one from heaven. Give us a demonstration, chains of evidence—chapter and verse—authority.

But simple men had decided the matter already. They knew very little of antiquity, church authority, and shadows of coming events which prophecy casts before. But their eyes saw the light, and their hearts felt the present God. Wise Pharisees and learned doctors said, to account for a wondrous miracle, "Give God the glory." But the poor unlettered man, whose blinded eye had for the first time looked on a face of love, replied, "Whether he be a sinner or no, I know not: one thing I know, that, whereas I was blind, now I see" (John 9:25).

The well-read Jews could not settle the literary question, whether the marks of His appearance coincided with the prophecies. But the Samaritans *felt* the life of God: "Now we believe, not because of thy saying: for we have heard him ourselves, and *know* that this is indeed the Christ" (John 4:42).

The Shepherd had come, and the sheep knew His voice. In all matters of eternal truth, the soul is before the intellect; the things of God are spiritually discerned. You know truth by being true; you recognize God by being like Him. The scribe comes and says, I will prove to you that this is sound doctrine by chapter and verse, by what the old and best writers say, by evidence such as convinces the intellect of an intelligent lawyer or juryman. Do you think the conviction of faith is gotten in that way?

Christ did not teach like the scribes. He spoke His truth. He said, "If any man believe not, I judge him not; the word which I have spoken, the same shall judge him in the last day." It was true, and the guilt of disbelieving it was not an error of the intellect, but a sin of the heart. Let us stand upright; let us be sure that the test of truth is the soul within us. Not at second-hand can we have assurance of what is divine and what is not—only at firsthand. The sheep of Christ hear His voice.

The third proof given by Christ was pastoral fidelity: *"I lay down my life for the sheep."* Now here is the doctrine of vicarious sacrifice: the sacrifice of one instead of another; life saved by the sacrifice of another life.

Most of us know the meager explanation of these words that satisfies the Unitarians. They say that Christ merely died as a martyr, in attestation of the truths He taught.

But you will observe the strength of the expression that we cannot explain away, "I lay down my *life for* [i.e., instead of] the sheep." If the Shepherd had not sacrificed Himself, the sheep must have been the sacrifice.

Observe, however, the suffering of Christ was not the same suffering as that from which He saved us. The suffering of Christ was death. But the suffering from which He redeemed us by death was more terrible than death. The pit into which He descended was the grave. But the pit in which we should have been lost forever was the pit of selfishness and despair.

Therefore St. Paul affirms, "If Christ be not raised, . . . ye are yet in your *sins"* (1 Cor. 15:17). If Christ's resurrection be a dream, and He be not risen from the grave of death, you are yet in the grave of guilt. He bore suffering to free us from what is worse than suffering—sin. He bore temporal death to save us from death everlasting. He gave His life an offering for sin to save the soul's eternal life.

Now in the text this sacrificing love of Christ is paralleled by the love of the Father to the Son. As He loved the sheep, so the Father had loved Him. Therefore the sacrifice of Christ is but a mirror of the love of God. The love of the Father to the Son is self-sacrificing love.

You know that shallow men make themselves merry with this doctrine. The sacrifice of God, they say, is a figment and an impossibility. Nevertheless, this parallel tells us that it is one of the deepest truths of all the universe. It is the profound truth which the ancient fathers endeavored to express in the doctrine

of the Trinity. For what is the love of the Father to the Son—
Himself yet not Himself—but the grand truth of eternal love los-
ing itself and finding itself again in the being of another? What
is it but the sublime expression of the unselfishness of God?

It is a profound, glorious truth. I wish I knew how to put it
in intelligible words. But if these words of Christ do not make
it intelligible to the heart, how can any words of mine? The
life of blessedness, the life of love, the life of sacrifice, the life
of God are identical. All love is sacrifice—the giving of life and
self for others. God's life is sacrifice—for the Father loves the
Son *as* the Son loves the sheep for whom He gave His life.

Whoever will humbly ponder upon this will, I think, understand the Atonement better than all theology can teach him.
O, my friends, leave men to quarrel as they will about the theology of the Atonement. Here in these words is the religion of
it—the blessed, all-satisfying religion for our hearts. The self-
sacrifice of Christ was the *satisfaction* to the Father.

How could the Father be *satisfied* with the death of Christ,
unless He saw in the sacrifice mirrored His own love? For God
can be satisfied only with that which is perfect as Himself. Agony
does not satisfy God—agony only satisfied Moloch. Nothing
satisfies God but the voluntary sacrifice of love.

The pain of Christ gave God no pleasure—only the love that
was tested by pain, the love of perfect obedience. He was obedient to death.

NOTES

The Preparation for Shepherding the Sheep

George Campbell Morgan (1863–1945) was the son of a British Baptist preacher and preached his first sermon when he was thirteen years old. He had no formal training for the ministry, but his tireless devotion to the study of the Bible helped him to become one of the leading Bible teachers of his day. Rejected by the Methodists, he was ordained into the Congregational ministry. He was associated with Dwight L. Moody in the Northfield Bible conferences and as an itinerant Bible teacher. He is best known as the pastor of the Westminster Chapel, London (1904–1917 and 1933–1943). During his second term, Dr. D. Martyn Lloyd-Jones was his associate.

Morgan published more than sixty books and booklets, and his sermons are found in *The Westminster Pulpit* (London: Hodder and Stoughton, 1906–1916). This sermon was given at the Westminster Bible Conference in Mundesley, Norfolk, and was found in their 1911 *Conference Report*. It can be found in another version in *The Westminster Pulpit,* volume 4.

3

The Preparation for Shepherding the Sheep

Feed my lambs. . . . Shepherd my sheep. . . . Feed my sheep.
(John 21:15–17)

IT HAS BEEN SAID THAT IN THESE WORDS our Lord handed the crosier to Peter, and they have constantly been interpreted as though their reference was solely to his work as an overseer of the flock of God gathered within the fold. I do not question for one single moment that the words have that application, but I entirely differ from those who would restrict their meaning in that particular way. I think we must interpret this passage, this charge of Jesus to Peter, in so far as it is figurative in language, by His perpetual use of the figure that He here employed.

In regard to this particular text our minds, I think, have been altogether too much obsessed by one very remarkable passage to be found in these gospel narratives. I refer to the passage in Matthew 25 where our Lord was speaking of a great day of judgment, when all nations shall be gathered before Him and when He will sit upon the throne, dividing asunder in the first place between the sheep and the goats. Basing our thinking constantly upon that one passage, a singularly solemn one, a most arresting one, it has taken such possession of our intellectual apprehension as to affect our thoughts whenever we come into the presence of this figure of speech. I pray you remember that here our Lord was speaking of an ultimate day, of a day of judgment. I do not believe that the particular prophecy in Matthew has any reference whatever to a judgment day when men will stand before Christ for individual judgment. I believe the value is entirely national. Let it, however, be granted for a moment that there may be individual applications and values, then I pray you to remember that this was the only occasion in the ministry of Jesus, so far as the records reveal, when He spoke of men as goats. Never until the final hour of finding the verdict, passing sentence, and sealing destiny did He so describe the sons of men. On the contrary, you will discover that His constant reference to all men was under the figure of sheep.

Mark the word in that matchless passage of Matthew's gospel in which, referring to the continuous and perpetual ministry of our Lord, he declared that passing through all the cities and villages He preached, He taught, He healed, and when He saw the multitudes He was moved with compassion for them because they were as *sheep* distressed, harried by wolves, fainting by the way. In that first phase of the threefold parable in the gospel of Luke He described His own ministry of redemption under the figure of the shepherd seeking the lost sheep. In those still deeper and more weighty words when He spoke of Himself as the Good Shepherd, He reminded the exclusive men who were about Him, "Other sheep I have, which are not of this fold: them also I must bring, and they shall hear my voice; and they shall become one fold, and one shepherd" (John 10:16). It is in the light of that constant method of our Master in His use of this figure that I think we must interpret His meaning when on that wonderful morning, across the flicker of the fire when the meal was over, He thrice challenged Peter, heard his threefold confession of love, and uttered to him these remarkable words: "Feed my lambs. . . . Shepherd my sheep. . . . Feed my sheep." Surely this is how Peter understood Him, for when long years after he wrote his letter, he thus described the saints to whom he wrote: "Ye were as sheep going astray; but are now returned unto the Shepherd and Bishop of your souls" (1 Peter 2:25).

I ask you, therefore, to come with me once more to the shores of the lake and listen to those words of our Lord addressed to Peter as the representative disciple. And I ask you to recognize that as our Lord uttered the words, He was thinking not only of the little group of disciples gathered about Him, the seven men who were there or the other four of the eleven who were away, or that multitude of five hundred scattered somewhere through the district. He stood that hour by the side of the lake, kissed with the glory of the rising sun, the One Great Shepherd, seeing far beyond that immediate group and embracing within His vision all the thronging multitudes of men through all the coming ages. Speaking to one man, and through one man, to all who should come into right relationship with Himself, He said, not of the immediate group but of those multitudes the vision of which moved His heart with compassion, "Feed my lambs. . . . Shepherd my sheep. . . . Feed my sheep."

These three words taken in that sense suggest to us the true work of the Christian church. Yet let me immediately say, beloved, that is not my burden tonight. It is not upon this that I propose to speak to you, as interesting, valuable, illuminative as these words are in that application. Through them there shines the glory of the vocation of the Christian church.

That which interests me in this final hour of the conference is the matter of the preparation necessary before our Lord can utter these words to an individual, or to a Christian church. And I am going to ask you to think with me as quietly and reverently as we may, and with all solemnity, of the hour in the experience of this man Peter at which our Lord was able to say this thing to him. For I submit to you that there is a great sequence, a great order in all the movement of our Lord's method with His own. The story of the training of the Twelve as I find it in these four gospels is a wonderful story full of light for us. Let us therefore center our attention upon this hour, this man, and our Master's dealings with him in order that we may know what preparation we need if we are to have any share in this great Christlike, godly work of feeding the lambs and shepherding the sheep.

Before we can dwell at any length intelligently upon the preparation necessary in the case of Peter, it is well that we should first recognize the assumptions of Jesus as revealed in these words. Oh, if we could but have heard them when He said them! That is the trouble with all interpretation, that it has to be done through the rough, coarse harshness of a human instrument. Oh that the brooding Spirit of God may bring to us the music of His own accents as we listen to these words. I believe as in the quiet hush we listen to hear Him say this thing, "Feed my lambs. . . . Shepherd my sheep. . . . Feed my sheep," the first impression made on the heart is that of His infinite compassion. The figure is in itself suggestive of the most tender relationship, of the most gracious attitude of which it is possible for us to think. We find warrant for saying so in that passage in Matthew's gospel. He saw the multitudes as sheep having no shepherd and, therefore, scattered, distressed. I need not tarry here. It has often been pointed out that the words themselves are pictures, and certainly, we do no violence to the story as we read it if instead of the direct word of translation we try and paint the picture. He beheld the multitudes as sheep fleeced, harried by wolves, and fainting by the way all for lack of a shepherd! "He was moved with compassion" (Matt. 9:36). We cannot understand it unless the wind of God breathe over us tonight. We are all so hard by comparison; we have so few tears. "He was moved with compassion"; that is the first note. It is Christ's affirmation of the infinite and profound agony of His soul in the presence of all human woe and weariness—My lambs, My sheep.

But there is another note. Not merely do I catch the accent of an infinite pity, I hear the ring of sovereign royalty. Hear again, "My lambs. . . . my sheep." It is the word of kingship.

It was Homer who once said, "All kings are shepherds." I venture to say that the word of Homer should be amended. All kings *ought* to be shepherds. This at least is true, that the idea of kingship in the divine library is always that of the shepherd. If Moses is to be the uncrowned king of the people during the period in which they merged into national constitution and consciousness, he must learn how to govern Israel forty years by being a shepherd in the backside of the desert for forty years. If David is to come into kingship, he must learn how to be the king of his people by fighting the lion and the bear and destroying them in the interests of his sheep. God's kings are always shepherds, and this King, standing out in the midst of the centuries, the one final King anointed and appointed of God, is the one supreme Shepherd of the human heart. While we dwell upon His compassion, let us never forget the assumption of royalty. We sing sometimes about the children:

> Then on each He setteth,
>   His own secret sign.
> They that have My Spirit,
>   These, saith He, are Mine.

Then let us remember this: there is no child that does not wear that sign—My lambs. Oh, the comfort of it, and the solemnity of it, My sheep. He is but repeating the tremendous word of the old prophetic declaration of Ezekiel and Jeremiah when men in captivity blamed their fathers for their present suffering and declared, "The fathers have eaten sour grapes, and the children's teeth are set on edge" (Ezek. 18:2). The prophets denied the false philosophy, and they denied by declaring, "Saith the Lord GOD, . . . all souls are mine" (vv. 3–4). And in this word of Jesus, when looking out over the vast multitudes—fleeced, harried, wandering, sin-sick, despoiled souls, He nevertheless said, "My sheep"—was the tone of His absolute sovereignty.

And yet there is another note sounding in it. A note

profounder and deeper at least for our hearts and understand-
ings, for this word was spoken to this man Peter after the Cross.
Before He had been to the cross He had uttered the words I
have quoted, "I am the good shepherd: the good shepherd
giveth his life for the sheep" (John 10:11). Then with a fine
and awful sarcasm are the words, "The hireling fleeth because
he is an hireling," but the Shepherd "layeth down His life for
the sheep." My lambs, My sheep, I have laid down My life for
them. I have entered into conflict with the grim and devilish
wolf to destroy him, and in the conflict I have died. They are
My lambs; they are My sheep. Thus, we have not merely the
note of compassion, not merely the note of sovereignty, but
the infinite music of saviorhood.

And yet there is one other note, the crowning note of all, for
remember this word was uttered after the Resurrection. He was
the risen Lord, mystic and mighty and merciful, but alive from
among the dead, as in that discourse in John He said, "I lay down
my life, that I might take it again" (v. 17). So now, having fulfilled the strange word, being alive from the dead, and demanding by the necessity of the case that His death must be interpreted
by His resurrection, He said, "My lambs. . . . my sheep."

Now with these assumptions in our minds, we come back
and look at this man. At what hour did Jesus say this to him, at
what place in the processes of his preparation? I want to make
this superlative, and in order to do so I affirm and pray you
ponder it at your leisure, that Christ could never have said this
to this man until this hour. The hour had arrived. The training was complete. The processes were over. Now he was ready,
and never before, for this great shepherd work. In order to
understand this, we need the whole history of the Master's
dealing with Peter, but it will suffice us for our present study if
we take the outstanding hours in that process of preparation.
You all know them. I am only going briefly over them that we
may understand in our study of them what is necessary before
Christ can say such a word as this to us. Let me name them
and then go over them quite briefly.

This man Peter had first felt the glamour of Christ's personality. Secondly, he had come to an hour in which he was convinced of the absolute supremacy of His Lord over all other teachers. Thirdly, he had faced the tragedy of the cross, felt the shame of it, and protesting against the vulgarity of it, had been angry. Finally, he had seen his Lord alive again from the dead. Not to use my own words, but to borrow Peter's, in the hour when he saw Him alive from the dead he was "begotten . . . again unto a lively hope" (1 Peter 1:3). I have but named, as you will see, the great crises in his spiritual experience through which he passed in preparation for this final commission.

First, the hour in which he felt the attraction, the irresistible charm of Christ's personality. Then the hour in which he came to the strong intellectual conviction of the absolute supremacy of his Master. Then the hour of protest and anger in the presence of the cross. And, finally, the dawn of that strange morning when even the tragic cross was transfigured into a tree of life and the perplexing mystery of blood became the herald of the final day of God. Through these experiences that man had passed before Christ said to him, "Feed my lambs" or "Shepherd my sheep." With each of these we might stay, but let us glance at them in the briefest way.

I have said that first of all Peter had passed under the spell of the matchless and wonderful personality of Jesus. You know the story, and those of you who know me best will know how well I love that story of his first meeting with Jesus, of the hour in which Andrew found his brother and brought him to Christ. The amazing thing in that story is this, that when Simon and Jesus first stood face to face, Simon did not utter a word. "[Andrew] first findeth his own brother Simon, and . . . brought him to Jesus. And when Jesus beheld him, he said, Thou art Simon the son of Jona: thou shalt be called Cephas [Rock]'" (John 1:41–42). Now, beloved, it is only as you remember this man, and the kind of man he was, that you begin to understand his silence. Why was he silent? Because he was surprised that day as he had never been surprised in his life before. Surprised that any man with eyes so full of penetrating light and so suffused with infinite emotion should look at him and suggest that he should ever be rock. That was the amazement. Simon Peter is in certain senses the greatest human on the pages of the New Testament. He is the elemental man, the man in whom all the elemental forces of humanity were present, but he lacked preciousness. What is preciousness? The welding into strength of the elements. That is Peter as Jesus first met him—elemental, intellectual. He asked more questions than any other disciple, and that is a demonstration of intellectual strength. Emotional, I need not argue it. Volitional, as witness his daring independence. Yes, but he was always blundering. Why? He lacked the principle that welds passion into dynamic, and the first time Jesus met him He looked into his eyes and said, "You are Simon, son of John. I know you, but you shall be rock."

Now this is not in the sermon, but I cannot forbear saying that this is the way to begin. If you want to win a man, look into his eyes and prophesy the highest possible for him and then begin to work toward the thing you have prophesied. Peter did not speak, but he followed Him. The Lord had gripped him. That is where true discipleship always begins, not in a theory of the Atonement understood or explained, but in the capture of a soul by Christ, even though men do not know the mystery of His person or hold any theory of His atoning work. That was the first thing.

But that was not enough to prepare this man for service. Two and a half years passed away, and they came to Caesarea Philippi, and there we need not tarry a moment longer than is necessary to hear what Peter said. The Lord asked, "Whom say ye that I am?" (Matt. 16:15; Mark 8:29; Luke 9:20). Now what did Peter say? Others had said that Jesus was Elijah; they had said He was Jeremiah; they had said he was John the Baptist; they had said He was one of the prophets. Peter declared, "Thou art the Christ" (Matt. 16:15; Mark 8:29; see Luke 9:20).

That meant, "No prophet are You, but the One for whose coming all prophets have been waiting. You are the One come to fulfill all the prophecy of our great history, gathering up the titles of the prophets, the Daystar, the Daysman, Shiloh, Emanuel. You are He." Or, to drop the word of Peter and to catch the thought of Peter, this is it, "No prophet are You, O Master, to be placed on a level with the rest. But You are the mysterious One toward whose coming they have looked, for the flash of whose advent upon the eastern sky souls have been waiting long. You are supreme. You are God's Messiah, His very Son." In that moment this man had taken a step beyond the response to the glamour of a personality; he had crowned Jesus intellectually as Lord and Master!

But even that does not prepare a man for feeding the lambs or for shepherding the sheep. Immediately our Lord brought him to the test, told him the secret of His church, and then began to show to His disciples that He must go to Jerusalem and suffer and be killed and the third day be raised again. Now would to God that we could understand Peter. Let us try and do so, for I clearly confess to you in my thinking and preaching I have often been unjust to him. It is quite easy to preach upon the frailty of this man and the folly of his refusal, but there is something deeper than all that. What troubled him? When at Caesarea Philippi he said to Jesus, "God help You, not that"; he meant, not the cross. Why not? No cross for You; You are the Messiah, the embodiment of the ideal, the incarnation of purity, God's revelation to men of all that is highest and noblest; no cross for You. The cross for You would be contrary to law and order and righteousness and godliness. That is what he meant. He was confronted with the horror of the thought that this Master of his, so full of light and love and purity and power, the peerless matchless One among the ages, that He could be the victim of sinning men. The tragedy of it made him hot and angry, and so it ought.

Now let us get right hold of this—so it ought! Ah, you say, the Lord rebuked him. Yes, rebuked him as He so often had to rebuke him, because he was not content to be silent in the presence of a mystery. Yet I thank God for the whole scene; for this tremendous word of Peter as well as for the stern rebuke of the Master's following method. In that moment Peter saw the horror of the cross, the tragedy of it; yes, I will use the word, the vulgarity of it! I am told that the cross is vulgar! So it is. But the vulgarity of the cross is the vulgarity of the sin that made it necessary, and Peter had not yet understood all the deep meaning of it. He simply stood and protested in agony of soul against the idea that the pure should be murdered, that the Master who to him was incarnate love and final authority could be mauled and murdered, as he himself did say presently in Pentecostal power, by the hands of men without law.

Yes, but that will not prepare a man for feeding the lambs. If a man shall get no farther than that, he will lack all that is necessary for feeding the lambs and shepherding the sheep. He must go farther, and the final step is that to which I have referred, and I shall illustrate it again by repeating Peter's own account of the effect produced on him. He said, "We were born again unto a living hope by the resurrection" (see 1 Peter 1:3). This means, "When they took our Master and nailed Him to the cross, we lost all hope. But when we saw Him alive beyond the cross, we discovered that it was necessary to reconsider the cross." He had told us all the way from Caesarea Philippi to Calvary that He must die. We had made our protest. We had been afraid, amazed. We had dropped out of sympathy with Him; He was so persistent. Even magnificent Thomas had said, "Let us go with Him and die with Him" (see John 11:16). It was a word of awful despair! And to the cross He did go. They nailed Him to the cross; and the very foundations seemed to have gone when they crucified Him. But, says Peter, Mary of Magdala came hurrying to the house of John.

Have you ever noticed where Peter spent that time? It was John who took him and cared for him in those dark days. Oh, I love that. When Mary of Magdala found the empty grave, while the other women went to others, Mary hurried to John and

Peter. John was taking care of the virgin mother, and I find Peter was there, too. Mary came to them, and they could not believe her. They ran to the sepulcher, and He was not there. But there they saw the grave clothes just as they had lain wrapped around the body, but the body was not there. And then Peter would have told you, He met me; He met me all alone. There is no record of the interview. What He said to me I cannot tell you, but what the actuality of His being alive did for me was this, I was born again to a living hope by the resurrection of Jesus from among the dead. When I met Him and found Him alive, I looked back and the brutal cross was transfused with light. The cursed tree was blossoming with the fruit of eternal life, and by the way of that tree I entered into life, for I knew what the cross meant when I saw Him alive. I will write it for you, said Peter, in this letter, "Who his own self bare our sins in his own body on the tree" (1 Peter 2:24).

To that man—captured first by the glamour of his Master's personality, brought to conviction of his Master's absolute supremacy, shocked by the vulgarity of the cross, reborn into a new outlook upon God and man and everything by the Resurrection—Jesus said, "Feed my lambs. . . . Shepherd my sheep." These are the preparations that are necessary if we are to do God's work in the world, and in this story of the happening by the shore that morning you will see that all those things are present. You have already discovered that the crises I have described exactly coincide with the assumptions of Jesus. The first note was the assumption of His compassion; that is what this man felt, the glamour of His personality. The second assumption was that of royalty, and to that the man had been brought when he said, "Thou art the Christ, the Son of the living God" (Matt. 16:16; see John 6:69). Next, His saviorhood, and the cross was in it, and to all that he came at Caesarea Philippi. The final note was that of resurrection power, and in the light of that resurrection the man had come to the full understanding. All those things were there. Mark where He began. Peter, you followed Me at first because you felt the attraction and the compulsion of My love. "Lovest thou Me?" (John 21:15–17). That is the first thing.

This is not the time and place, and yet one dare not pass it over, to remind you that the word Jesus used for love and the word Peter used are not the same. The Revised Version has drawn attention to it by this most remarkable note in the margin. It says the words which Jesus used for *love* and Peter used for *love* are not identical. Was there ever a more brilliant way of making darkness visible than that? It leaves you where you were. The ordinary reader is not helped by that. Those who read the Greek understand it immediately. Two words: Christ's word *agapeo,* and Peter's word *phileo.* Who shall draw a distinction between them? It is very difficult. The word that Christ used was a word for love on the highest level. Love that is not merely emotion, but love that is emotional and intellectual and volitional; love in which the whole man acts deliberately. Peter's word was the word of the emotion. Christ said to him, "Lovest thou me?" with this highest love; Peter said, "Lord, Thou knowest I [fondly] love thee" (v. 15). Yes, but Peter, do you love Me with this illuminated love, this intellectual apprehension and volitional consent. "Lord, Thou knowest that I [fondly] love thee" (v. 16). Now the third time Jesus came down to his word. This is why he was grieved, because Jesus descended when Peter could not climb to the high word. But yet what matchless grace! If this man cannot climb to the higher, Christ will be content with the lower, if love is in it. "Lovest thou me [fondly]" (v. 17).

That is the first thing. That is the first thing if you are going out from this conference to do anything for the Master. "Do you love Me?" He says. Now God forgive us that we take that question and bandy it about in this respect, as though it were of all questions the easiest. Let me raise no smile. Affairs of the heart are the most sacred things of human life, next to relation to God. Is there anything more sacred than when the question is asked, "Lovest thou me?" and everything for life depends upon it as between man and woman? That is a low level. Climb a little higher. This One Jesus, lover of my soul, comes wooing workers, and that is His first question, supreme and all-embracing in many respects, "Lovest thou me?" And unless we can say to Him, "Lord, thou knowest that I [fondly] love thee," we cannot feed His lambs and cannot shepherd His sheep. There is no other motive that will keep us at the hard difficult work than that of love for Christ.

My dear friend Dr. Scofield was telling me that a girl, a member of his church, was going out to China as a missionary. Before she left he said to her, "Well, I suppose you are going to China because you love these Chinese." She was a fine, saintly, truthful girl, and replied, "Oh no, Dr. Scofield, I do not love them at all. I do not like them." He said, "Then why are you going?" Then the strong voice, carrying the tremor of a great devotion, replied, "I am going because I love my Lord, and He has sent me." That is it. Seven years after she came home, and said, "Doctor, do you remember what I said when I was going?" "Very well," he replied. "Well, I want to tell you now that I love them, too." Yes, but you do not start that way, and I think that is why so few people dare to touch the corruption and the sin and the misery of men at home or abroad. You are not to go first because you love them, but because you love Him. That is the first thing.

And next in this picture, what have I? Peter, you came to conviction of My supremacy. I want you to prove your loyalty by sharing the function of My royalty. What a wonderful word is this. I am the Good Shepherd. Peter, help Me shepherd My sheep. Prove your loyalty to Me as supreme by coming into partnership with Me, into the royalty that seeks and saves and folds the flock. Did ever king think of anything like that before? Would any other king use such a method to demonstrate the loyalty of his subjects, that of asking them to share in the prerogative of his royalty? This is a very supreme matter—you and I can never really feed His lambs or shepherd His sheep until we are quite sure about His absolute supremacy. If I merely discourse on comparative religions in the pulpit, I can do no shepherding of lost sheep. If I am not sure whether after all it is not better to leave those distant nations to Confucius and Buddha and Zoroaster, and the rest of them, well then, in God's name let me stay at home! Unless we have looked into His eyes and said, "O King most wonderful, even though as yet we do not understand all the mystery of Your Person, You are peerless, alone, absolutely supreme. We had better keep our hands off the lambs and off the sheep."

And further. Peter, said Jesus, "When thou wast young, thou girdedst thyself, and walkedst whither thou wouldest: but when thou shalt be old, thou shalt stretch forth thy hands, and another shall gird thee, and carry thee whither thou wouldest not" (John 21:18). He was calling Peter to his cross. He was saying to him, Peter, if you are to have real fellowship with Me in My work, you also will have to walk the pathway that will culminate in the cross. You must be content to give yourself over to that treatment which is unrighteous, in order that by that sacrifice of self you may communicate regenerative dynamic to the very men who lay murderous hands upon you. That is the deep, profound word of the cross for the Christian soul. We are to go out, without the camp with Him, and no man will ever come into full fellowship with Christ until he sees first the tragedy of the cross— that it was unwarranted, that it was evil on the human level. Peter saw it, saw it in a flash and a flame of glory by resurrection and by Pentecost. When he began to preach after Pentecost, listen to what he said about the cross: "Him, being delivered by the determinate counsel and foreknowledge of God, ye have taken, and by wicked hands have crucified and slain" (Acts 2:23). On the one hand human lawlessness against which all the protest of the soul must be made. And, my friends, you and I never understand sin until we look at that cross. The hour in which we attempt to account for sin in other ways than by examining it in the light of the cross, the agony, the vulgarity, the shame of it, is the hour of our failure to do God's work in the world.

But thank God, that is not the last word in my story. John in his gospel—and I am not criticizing him—introduces a parenthesis there in order that we may be quite sure what Jesus meant. He said, "This spake he, signifying by what death he should glorify God" (John 21:19). Then he goes on to write, "And when he had spoken this, he saith unto him, Follow me" (v. 19). Do not forget that as a matter of fact our Lord said, "Follow Me immediately in connection with the word of the cross." So that for our understanding I shall for one moment omit John's parenthesis and listen again to what Jesus said to Peter, "When thou wast young, thou girdedst thyself, and walkedst whither thou wouldest: but when thou shalt be old, thou shalt stretch forth thy hands, and another shall gird thee, and carry thee whither thou wouldest not. . . . Follow me" (vv. 18–19). Peter, you were afraid of the cross, trembled before it, were shocked by it, but you must come that way also. The servant is not above his Lord. If you are to enter into the fellowship of My work, you must take up your cross and follow Me. Peter, you are afraid of the cross, but you know what it meant to Me. I came to the cross, but I went beyond it. I went to death, but I emerged from it. I walked the *via dolorosa* that culminated in Golgotha, but I came to the glory of the Easter morning. Follow Me! Follow Me! If you suffer with Me, you shall reign with Me. If you die with Me, you shall rise with Me and come to the throne of power with Me.

That is the way in which a man is ready to feed the lambs, to shepherd the sheep. My friends, where are we? We have said it over and over again in this conference. Speaker after speaker I have noticed has referred to the fact that the real value of a gathering like this is found when it is over and we are back again in our own churches, confronting our own difficulties, and mixing and merging with men and women in the everyday life of the home and the church; or, when we are presently back again in the distant places of the world.

What is the Master saying to us tonight? He wants to say to me—and O God, help us to do business here about this matter— He wants to say to me, He wants to say to you, "Feed my lambs. . . . Shepherd my sheep. . . . Feed my sheep. These fleeced and harried multitudes of men that are despoiled and distressed, shepherd them, gather them." Can we do it? Oh, if we love Him, if He is the absolute Lord of our life, if we have seen the tragedy of the cross and measured sin by that cross. If we have seen the cross transfigured by the Resurrection and are willing to follow, then we may go back again to feed the lambs, to shepherd the sheep. May that Great Shepherd of the sheep speak His own word to our hearts that we may go to the city, to the village, to the dark lands that lie beyond, to feed the lambs, shepherd the sheep, for His own name's sake.

The Lord Is My Shepherd

James McGinlay (1901–1958) was a gifted evangelist and Bible conference speaker whose Scottish accent and humor endeared him to congregations throughout the United States and Canada. He pastored Baptist churches in Brooklyn, New York, and London, Ontario, Canada, and published several books of sermons. Among those that best demonstrate his unique homiletical style are *Heaven's Jewelry; Not Now, but Afterwards;* and *The Birthday of Souls.* Dr. Herbert Lockyer Sr. called McGinlay "a born orator" whose preaching was "unique and gospel-drenched."

This sermon was taken from *Heaven's Jewelry,* which was copywritten and published by W. B. Eerdmans Company in 1946. Used by permission; all rights reserved.

4

The Lord Is My Shepherd

The LORD is my shepherd; I shall not want. He maketh me to lie
down in green pastures: he leadeth me beside the still waters.
He restoreth my soul: he leadeth me in the paths of righteousness
for his name's sake. Yea, though I walk through the valley of the
shadow of death, I will fear no evil: for thou art with me;
thy rod and thy staff they comfort me. Thou preparest a table
before me in the presence of mine enemies: thou anointest my
head with oil; my cup runneth over. Surely goodness and mercy
shall follow me all the days of my life: and I will dwell in the
house of the LORD for ever. (Psalm 23)

NEVER SHALL I FORGET A PERIOD IN MY PECULIAR LIFE through which
I never want to pass again. I was four thousand miles from my
native land, separated from loved ones, with no friends, no
home, and no God.

Walking along the street from my room on a cold, dark,
wintry night, passing an open doorway, I would peep in. There
in the glowing light I would see the father and mother, the boys
and girls playing and laughing together. Then the door would
shut, yet the memory of what I saw lingered with me for days
and led me to believe that surely a better day was coming for
me by and by.

There is a likeness between my experience and the truth

expressed in the Twenty-third Psalm. To me, this psalm is simply the opening of the door to our eternal inheritance, which
brings to my heart sweet peace.

You and I are away from home. Heaven is our abode. Our
Father lives there and most of our loved ones, if not all of them,
are there even now. The night of sin is dark. The breath of a
Christ-hating world is chilly on our cheeks. There is no rest
for the sole of our feet, and we have nowhere to lay our head.
Thank God for the day when David opened the door and,
through a crack of six short verses in the Twenty-third Psalm,
enabled us to see that which is ours by God's grace.

The position of this psalm in the Word of God is of peculiar significance. It comes after the Twenty-second, which is the
psalm of the cross—and there are no shepherds, green pastures,
or still waters on the other side of Calvary.

It is only after we understand the cry of the Savior, "My God,
my God, why hast thou forsaken me?" (Ps. 22:1) that we can
say, "The Lord is my shepherd, I shall not want." We must
know, experimentally, the meaning of the Twenty-second Psalm
before we can enjoy the Twenty-third. Unless you are a blood-
bought child of God, David's shepherd psalm will be to you a
tasteless, empty thing.

The Lord Is My Shepherd

Doesn't the condescension of our great God humble us to
the dust? How many of us would choose for our life's work
the vocation of a shepherd? Yet, for our sakes, He who is God
over all, blessed forever, became just that.

David was a shepherd. It may have been that it was while he
was sitting under a tree one day watching his sheep that he wrote
this psalm. He realized the trials and worries of a shepherd. He
knew what a task was his to keep the sheep on the beaten track.
But poor David also knew what a weakling he was, how prone
to go astray, and how utterly incapable of looking after himself;
so he says, "The Lord is my shepherd." Is the Lord your Shepherd? Then if He is, you are one of His sheep.

A sheep always signifies possession. It is not a wild mountain goat, or a wolf, or a fox. It is a sheep. It belongs to its owner and is answerable to its shepherd. No man or woman has a right to say, "The LORD is my shepherd" who is not living like a sheep. When we Christians scratch each other like wolves or wild cats, or tear each other at the slightest provocation, don't you think we are making goats of ourselves. Instead of having a shepherd, we need a drover? Eh? Before we pass from that, look at the word *my*.

"The Lord is my shepherd." It is true that the Lord is the Shepherd of the whole flock scattered the world over, but hallelujah, He is mine! If He is a Shepherd to nobody else, He is a Shepherd to me. That's what David said. He looks after me; He cares for me; He is my very own. Oh, discouraged saint, your friends have turned you down, but He has not. He is your very own precious Shepherd, and you are His sheep.

"I shall not want." Of course, if we are His and He is ours, we shall not want. The business of a conscientious shepherd is to find the wherewithal to feed his sheep. How long do you think it will take us to learn this lesson, and stop our skipping over the Devil's walls and fences for help, when our Shepherd is anxious to supply our every need? Millionaires will come to want. Rich land owners will lose their holdings, but we shall never want.

Does He not feed the ravens and clothe the lilies? Then surely, in the name of all that is reasonable, the Good Shepherd will not let His own sheep want while He is looking after the birds and the flowers. Let the soldier trust his sword, the scholar his learning, the rich man his wealth; but we will trust our God. The sinner is always in want, for his heart is crying out day and night for that which he does not have, while the child of God who has learned the heavenly secret dwells in the palace of contentment.

You have heard of the poor woman, lying on a pallet of straw on a garret floor. Somebody brought her a loaf of stale bread, and after the donor had gone, she held it up. As she cuddled

it to her breast, she said, "Imagine, all this and Jesus into the
bargain!"

He Maketh Me to Lie Down in Green Pastures:
He Leadeth Me Beside the Still Waters

There are two elements governing the make up of a Christian life. We have to eat and work. What are those green pastures through which our Shepherd leads us? They are His
precious Word. That is what feeds our souls and nourishes our
spiritual life. How empty a sheep would become if day after
day it sojourns in a dried-up, barren field with no fresh grass
to eat! Have you stopped reading your Bible?

Can you see this picture? The sheep are led into a beautiful
meadow of nice green luscious grass. After a long march over
rocky places, they are led into the green pastures. Now when
they are coming along, one sheep bumps the other with its
horn. Another sheep steps on the other sheep's toe. One of
the ewes sticks its tongue out at one of the other ewe's lambs.
So now, they have reached the green pastures, and because they
have had a little bit of a squabble beforehand, they lie there
and refuse to eat.

Do you know that the Devil loves to get God's sheep wran-
gling with each other until he has spoiled their appetite for
God's green pastures? Do you have a grudge in your heart today so that you cannot enjoy this message? Do you lie down in
the green pastures, or do you just walk through them? The
difference between lying down in the pastures instead of merely
walking through them is that when you lie down in them, you
can eat without even bending your head. Some Christians read
the Bible and believe every word of it, but they never lay hold
upon the promises and make them practical in their lives.

It is the shepherd who causes the sheep to lie down in green
pastures, and it is the Lord who causes us to enjoy the preciousness of His Word.

The second part of a Christian's life consists in activity. We
ought to have in our spiritual lives a combination of the traits

of Martha and Mary. Mary studied and Martha served. So we, too, should be at the feet of Jesus, learning of Him the one moment and up and doing the next. Let us not just go to church and study the Bible and go home. Let us see what we can do to get things done. The sheep are lying in the green pastures one moment, and the next, they are being led by the still waters. We must eat and then journey on toward holiness and service. Are you more spiritual today than you were last year? Are you more easily provoked to wrath than you were last month? Then you are not allowing God to lead you beside the still waters. For still waters run deep, and so will our Christian lives, if we allow the Shepherd to lead us. Moses drives us by the law of Sinai, but Christ leads us by the passion of Calvary.

He Restoreth My Soul

Is your soul sorrowful today, or are you cast down? He will restore it and send you away happy. He is ready and willing to lift the clouds and let the sunshine in.

Have you backslidden? I can't help you, but, thank God, He can. If He is your Shepherd, and you have wandered away from Him, He will restore you.

"He leadeth me in the paths of righteousness." How many of God's children are there who would give everything they have to walk daily in the paths of righteousness? You notice David says, "He leadeth me." He did not say, "He driveth me." Leading implies consent; driving involves compulsion, and God never compels any of us to do the thing that is right. If we want to walk in righteousness, all we do is look to Him and He will do for us what only a shepherd can do—lead us "in the paths of righteousness."

Can't you see a shepherd with a great herd of sheep? They are coming down from the hills. I remember as a boy how that some sheep always come trotting along beside the shepherd. Others are "on their own." They know the way, and when they come to the stream, they go hollus bollus in over the neck. Look at these sheep that are near to the shepherd. What do they do? They look to him for guidance, and he carefully leads them across the narrow place. Then here comes a little weak lamb, God love it, wobbling along on its wee shaky pins. How on earth is it going to cross that stream? All it does is look up into the face of the shepherd and bleat. The shepherd picks it up and carries it safely over. So in a church. There are some church people who graduate from the school of sitting at the feet of Jesus, and all they do is forge ahead, getting offices and doing things. The next thing you know, they are away from God and from the paths of righteousness. Oh, let us allow Him to lead us for His name's sake.

Yea, Though I Walk Through the Valley of the Shadow of Death, I Will Fear No Evil: for Thou Art with Me; Thy Rod and Thy Staff They Comfort Me

"Yea, though I walk . . ." You notice that David pictures the closing days of a Christian as a quiet walk—no impatient scurry or flurry, but a steady walk. Dear friends, live for God so that when you come to the end, there is no worry. Some Christians spend their lifetime backsliding so far from God that when the end comes, they are not conscious as to whether they are right or wrong.

The saint who lives in daily and hourly communion with God is in no excited hurry when he comes to die. Death to him is a steady advance. He knows every step of the way and has prepared for it. The last days of a Christian ought to be the most peaceful of all. The mountain is now bleak, but the valley is all aglow.

You notice, too, that David does not say we walk *in* the valley of the shadow of death. No. He says we walk *through* it. Praise God, it is a continuous journey and we go out at the other end to life and immortality.

Again, he does not call it the valley of death. He says the valley of the *shadow* of death. Praise God, there is no death to the Christian; it is just a shadow. How can death have a shadow? Well, they say that there can be no shadow without a light, and so when we go through the valley, Christ the light will be with us. Death is only a vague shadow of what it used to be before we knew the Savior.

The substance of death has been removed and all that is left is the shadow. Nobody is afraid of a shadow. The shadow of a dog cannot bite you. The shadow of a sword cannot kill you. Neither can the shadow of death harm you. "For thou [the Lord] art with me; thy rod and thy staff they comfort me."

Thou Preparest a Table Before Me
in the Presence of Mine Enemies

Without straining the metaphor, I am sure we are safe in saying that the table of the Twenty-third Psalm stands for the whole provision our Shepherd has made for us: provision for joy as well as sorrow, for time as well as for eternity. In fact, the table is none other than Christ Himself. He is our salvation. In Him, we have justification, adoption, and sanctification. Yea, everything we need is found in Christ.

> He is the treasure of our soul,
>   The source of lasting joy.
> A joy that want shall not impair,
>   Nor death itself destroy.

"*In the presence of mine enemies.*" This is our "safety, certainty, and enjoyment." While here in this world below, we Christians are in enemy territory. In heaven, there will be no enemies to oppose us, and for that we ought to thank God. However, until we arrive in that glorious land, we are continually opposed by our foes—many of them on the inside. Look at them, the beggars! See the hateful gleam in their eyes—old sins, fears, and temptations.

"We'll have you yet," they cry. "In spite of those Calvary nails that shed blood and the promises of the Bible, we will win you back."

Ouch! Let them hiss. What do we care? Let them fuss and fume all they want; we have escaped their malice. We now belong to Christ. Not a hair of our head shall perish. No weapon that is formed against us shall prosper. The saints in glory may be a lot happier there than we are, but they are no safer. They are no nearer, nor no dearer to Christ, nor held more securely in the keeping of Christ than we are down here in the presence of our enemies.

"Thou anointest my head with oil; my cup runneth over." This surely suggests that there is nothing stingy or small in what we call God's salvation. We worship and trust a God who is too big in Himself to do anything little for us. It is true that in our unregenerate days we were poor, helpless, wandering sinners, but now we are kings and priests and princes. We are heirs of God and joint-heirs with Jesus Christ. How thrilled we ought to be with God's forgiveness! The burden and the gloom of our sin are gone, yes, gone completely and forever.

If you are prone to doubt that ours is an overflowing salvation, just contrast it with human forgiveness. There is nothing overflowing about that. Men seldom forgive with a kiss; they forgive with a kick, and then consider you unethical if you don't come up for more. They bury the hatchet, all right, but leave the handle sticking out of the ground for future use. To forgive, to forget, to remember no more, to cast behind the back and into the depths of the sea forever—these are the elements of an overflowing salvation. God not only pardons; He *abundantly* pardons.

There are preachers today who would give us a revised version of the experiences of the prodigal son. It would run something like this: "The prodigal came home. But the father, in the interest of the family and society at large, restrained his emotions and said, 'Well, black sheep, you are back, I see. I thought you would come home when you had enough of the wicked world. Let me warn you, however, that I shall stand for no more scandal in our family. The professional future of your elder brother must not be jeopardized by a scalawag like you. Take a bath, now, and I'll have one of the servants spray you with a good powerful disinfectant before you dress. Then go around to the kitchen and see if the cook has any cold pork and beans for your repast.'"

O God, save us from such religious mockery! We are cursed with a false refinement in our churches, while the world outside is languishing for the knowledge of an overflowing cup. It must bring sorrow to the heart of Christ as He listens on a Sunday morning to the dry, dying devotion of a million souls all over the land for whose redemption He shed His precious blood. In heaven, however, the overflowing cup will be answered by the overflowing song.

Surely Goodness and Mercy Shall Follow Me All the Days of My Life: and I Will Dwell in the House of the Lord Forever

"Goodness and mercy shall follow me all the days of my life." Then what comes next? Science cannot tell us, philosophy cannot explain to us, nor can poetry reveal the answer. Only our faith in God's Word can finish the sentence, "And I will dwell in the house of the Lord for ever."

The Lord who inspired David to write this psalm looks down through the days of a Christian life, and He sees an element of goodness and mercy in it. We say, "Well, I have had some good days. My wedding day was one of them. What a thrill, when I carried my bride across the threshold of our new home, where, together, we spent many happy days!" But what about the day you walked behind her casket, out of that happy home to the cemetery? Don't forget now, it is *"all* the days of my life"—the good days and the bad days, the sick days and the well days, the rich days and the poor days, the days you won and the days you lost. Let's be accurate in our bookkeeping.

I would like to address David now that his life is over. I would say, "David, you expected goodness and mercy to follow you all the days of your life. Do you still believe it?"

I hear him reply, "Yes, there were goodness and mercy in my happy boyhood days at Bethlehem and goodness and mercy the day I killed Goliath. Then there were the dark days when I was hunted like a wild beast with a price on my head, and the day when I threw up my hands and said, 'It is all over. I shall perish by the hand of Saul' [see 1 Sam. 27:1]. I didn't perish, but Saul did."

David bows his head and, with a blush, he mentions the dark days associated with Bathsheba, and the even darker days when he planned Uriah's death. Then he speaks of the day the baby died, and following that the funeral day. "Yes," says David, "now that I am in heaven and look back over my life, I still believe, but more firmly than when I wrote it in the Twenty-third Psalm, that 'goodness and mercy shall [and did] follow me all the days of my life.'"

Friends, we don't require David's testimony to bear out this truth. We have our own. I have had my bright days and my dark days, my happy days and my sad days, and so have you. In fact, as I pen these words, I have only two more days before entering a hospital in Glendale, California, to submit once more to the knife of surgery. My only regret is my unworthiness and comparative uselessness to the Christ who has been and still is my dearest Friend.

With David, I look back over my life and I can honestly say that goodness and mercy have followed me, and with a halle-lujah I go all the way with David to the end of the psalm—"I will dwell in the house of the LORD for ever."

Should the Lord tarry long enough to permit our departure from this life by way of the tomb, an appropriate swan song for our deathbed might well be that dear old hymn of the church:

> When all Thy mercies, O my God,
>   My rising soul surveys.
> Transported with the view, I'm lost
>   In wonder, love, and praise!
>
> Oh, how shall words, with equal warmth,
>   The gratitude declare,

That grows within my ravished heart?
  But Thou canst read it there.

When nature fails, and day and night
  Divide Thy works no more,
My ever grateful heart, O Lord,
  Thy goodness shall adore.

To all eternity, to Thee
  A joyful song I'll raise;
For, oh, eternity's too short
  To utter all Thy praise!

Even so, as in our illustration at the beginning of our psalm, the door closes, but, bless God, we have had a glimpse of our "Home, Sweet Home."

The Shepherd King of Israel

Alexander Maclaren (1826–1910) was one of Great Britain's most famous preachers. While pastoring the Union Chapel, Manchester (1858–1903), he became known as "the prince of expository preachers." Rarely active in denominational or civic affairs, Maclaren invested his time in studying the Word in the original languages and in sharing its truths with others in sermons that are still models of effective expository preaching. He published a number of books of sermons, and the climax of his ministry was publication of the monumental *Expositions of Holy Scripture*.

This message was taken from *Sermons Preached in Manchester: First Series,* published by Funk and Wagnalls in 1902.

5

The Shepherd King of Israel

The LORD is my shepherd; I shall not want. He maketh me to lie
down in green pastures: he leadeth me beside the still waters.
He restoreth my soul: he leadeth me in the paths of righteousness
for his name's sake. Yea, though I walk through the valley of the
shadow of death, I will fear no evil: for thou art with me;
thy rod and thy staff they comfort me. Thou preparest a table
before me in the presence of mine enemies: thou anointest my
head with oil; my cup runneth over. Surely goodness and mercy
shall follow me all the days of my life: and I will dwell in the
house of the LORD for ever. (Psalm 23)

THE KING WHO HAD BEEN THE SHEPHERD BOY and had been taken from
the quiet sheep cotes to rule over Israel sings this little psalm of
Him who is the true Shepherd and King of men. We do not know
at what period of David's life it was written, but it sounds as if it
were the work of his later years. There is a fullness of experience
about it, and a tone of subdued, quiet confidence, which speaks
of a heart mellowed by years, and of a faith made sober by many
a trial. A young man would not write so calmly, and a life which
was just opening would not afford material for such a record of
God's guardianship in all changing circumstances.

If, then, we think of the psalm as the work of David's later
years, is it not very beautiful to see the old king looking back

with such vivid and loving remembrance to his childhood's occupation, and bringing up again to memory in his palace the green valleys, the gentle streams, the dark glens where he had led his flocks in the old days? Is it not very beautiful to see him traversing all the stormy years of warfare and rebellion, of crime and sorrow, which lay between, and finding in all God's guardian presence and gracious guidance? The faith that looks back and says, "It is all very good," is not less than that which looks forward and says, "Surely goodness and mercy shall follow me all the days of my life."

There is nothing difficult of understanding in the psalm. The train of thought is clear and obvious. The experiences that it details are common; the emotions it expresses simple and familiar. The tears that have been dried and the fears that have been dissipated by this old song, the love and thankfulness that have found in them their best expression, prove the worth of its simple words. It lives in most of our memories. Let us try to vivify it in our hearts by pondering it for a little while together now.

The psalm falls into two halves, in both of which the same general thought of God's guardian care is presented, though under different illustrations and with some variety of detail. The first half sets Him forth as a Shepherd and us as the sheep of His pasture. The second gives Him as the Host, and us as the guests at His table and the dwellers in His house.

The Divine Shepherd and the Leading of His Flock

First, then, consider that picture of the divine Shepherd and His leading of His flock. It occupies the first four verses of the psalm. There is a double progress of thought in it. It rises from memories of the past and experiences of the present care of God to hope for the future. *"The Lord is my shepherd. . . . I will fear no evil."* Then besides this progress from what was and is to what will be, there is another string, so to speak, on which the gems are threaded. The various methods of God's leading of His flock, or rather, we should say, the various regions into which He leads them are described in order. These are *rest, work, sorrow.* This series is so combined with the order of time already adverted to as that the past and the present are considered as the regions of rest and of work, while the future is anticipated as having in it the valley of the shadow of death.

First, God leads His sheep into rest. *"He maketh me to lie down in green pastures: he leadeth me beside the still waters."* It is the hot noontide, and the desert lies baking in the awful glare and every stone on the hills of Judea burns the foot that touches it. But in that panting, breathless hour, here is a little green glen with a quiet brooklet and a moist lush herbage all along its course with great stones that fling a black shadow over the dewy grass at their base. There would the shepherd lead his flock while the "sunbeams, like swords" are piercing everything beyond that hidden covert. Sweet silence broods there. The sheep feed and drink and couch in cool lairs until he calls them forth again. So God leads His children.

The psalm puts the rest and refreshment *first,* as being the most marked characteristic of God's dealings. After all, it is so. The years are years of unbroken continuity of outward blessings. The reign of afflictions is ordinarily measured by days. Weeping endures for a night. It is a rainy climate where half the days have rain in them. That is an unusually troubled life of which it can, with any truth, be affirmed that there has been as much darkness as sunshine in it.

But it is not mainly of outward blessings that the psalmist is thinking. They are precious chiefly as emblems of the better spiritual gifts. It is not an accommodation of his words. But it is the appreciation of their truest spirit when we look upon them, as the instinct of devout hearts has ever done, as expressing both God's gift of temporal mercies and His gift of spiritual good, of which higher gift all the lower are meant to be significant and symbolic. Thus regarded, the image describes the sweet rest of the soul in communion with God, in whom alone the hungry heart finds food that satisfies, and from whom alone the thirsty soul drinks draughts deep and limpid enough.

This rest and refreshment has for its consequence the restoration of the soul, which includes in it both the invigoration of the natural life by the outward sort of these blessings, and the quickening and restoration of the spiritual life by the inward feeding upon God and repose in Him.

The soul thus restored is then led on another stage. *"He leadeth me in the paths of righteousness for his name's sake."* That is to say, God guides us into work.

The quiet mercies of the preceding verse are not in themselves the end of our Shepherd's guidance. They are means to an end, and that is—work. Life is not a fold for the sheep to lie down in but a road for them to walk on. All our blessings of every sort are indeed given us for our delight. They will never fit us for the duties for which they are intended to prepare us, unless they first be thoroughly enjoyed. The highest good they yield is only reached through the lower one. But, then, when joy fills the heart and life is bounding in the veins, we have to learn that these are granted not for pleasure only but for pleasure in order to power. We get them not to let them pass away like waste steam puffed into empty air, but that we may use them to drive the wheels of life. The waters of happiness are not for a luxurious bath where a man may lie until, like flax steeped too long, the very fiber be rotted out of him. A quick plunge will brace him, and he will come out refreshed for work. Rest is to fit for work; work is to sweeten rest.

All this is emphatically true of the spiritual life. Its seasons of communion and hours on the mount are to prepare for the sore sad work in the plain. He is not the wisest disciple who tries to make the Mount of Transfiguration the abiding place for himself and his Lord.

It is not well that our chief object should be to enjoy the consolations of religion. It is better to seek first to do the duties enjoined by religion. Our first question should not be, "How may I enjoy God?" but, "How may I glorify Him?" "A single eye to His glory" means that even our comfort and joy in religious exercises shall be subordinated and, if need were, postponed to the doing of His will. While, on the one hand, there is no more certain means of enjoying Him than that of humbly seeking to walk in the ways of His commandments, on the other hand, there is nothing more evanescent in its nature than a mere emotion, even though it be that of joy in God unless it be turned into a spring of action for God. Such emotions, like photographs, vanish from the heart unless they be fixed. Work for God is the way to fix them. Joy in God is the strength of work for God, but work for God is the perpetuation of joy in God.

Here is the figurative expression of the great evangelical principle, that works of righteousness must follow, not precede, the restoration of the soul. We are justified not by works but for works. Or, as the apostle puts it in a passage that sounds like an echo of this psalm, we are "created in Christ Jesus unto good works, which God hath before ordained *that we should walk in them*" (Eph. 2:10). The basis of obedience is the sense of salvation. We work not *for* the assurance of acceptance and forgiveness, but *from* it. First the restored soul, then the paths of righteousness for His name's sake who has restored me, and restored me that I may be like Him.

But there is yet another region through which the varied experience of the Christian carries him besides those of rest and of work. God leads His people through sorrow. "Yea, *though I walk through the valley of the shadow of death, I will fear no evil.*"

The "valley of the shadow of death" does not only mean the dark approach to the dark dissolution of soul and body, but any and every gloomy valley of weeping through which we have to pass. Such sunless gorges we have all to traverse at some time or other. It is striking that the psalmist puts the sorrow, which is as certainly characteristic of our lot as the rest or the work, into the future. Looking back he sees none. Memory has softened down all the past into one uniform tone, as the mellowing distance wraps in one solemn purple the mountains which, when close to them, have many a barren rock and gloomy rift. All behind is good. And, building on this hope, he looks forward with calmness and feels that no evil shall befall.

But it is never given to human heart to meditate of the future without some foreboding. And when "hope enchanted smiles" with the light of the future in her blue eyes, there is ever something awful in their depths, as if they saw some dark visions behind the beauty. Some evils may come; some will probably come; one at least is sure to come. However bright may be the path, somewhere on it, perhaps just round that turn, sits the "shadow feared of man." So there is never pure hope in any heart that wisely considers the future. But to the Christian heart there may be this—the conviction that sorrow, when it comes, will not be evil because God will be with us. The conviction that the hand that guides us into the dark valley will guide us through it and up out of it. Yes, strange as it may sound, the presence of Him who sends the sorrow is the best help to bear it. The assurance that the hand which strikes is the hand which binds up makes the stroke a blessing, sucks the poison out of the wound of sorrow, and turns the rod that smites into the staff to lean on.

God as the Host and Us as the Guests and Dwellers

The second portion of this psalm gives us substantially the same thoughts under a different image. Consider God as the Host and us as the guests at His table and the dwellers in His house. In this illustration, which includes the remaining verses, we have, as before, the food and rest, the journey and the suffering. We have also, as before, memory and present experience issuing in hope. But it is all intensified. The necessity and the mercy alike are presented in brighter colors. The want is greater, the supply greater, the hope for the future on earth brighter. Above all, while the former set of images stopped at the side of the grave and simply refused to fear, here the vision goes on beyond the earthly end. As the hope comes brightly out that all the weary wanderings will end in the peace of the Father's house, the absence of fear is changed into the presence of triumphant confidence and the resignation, which, at the most, simply bore to look unfaltering into the depth of the narrow house, becomes the faith that plainly sees the open gate of the everlasting home.

God supplies our wants in the very midst of strife. *"Thou preparest a table before me in the presence of mine enemies: thou anointest my head with oil; my cup runneth over."* Before, it was food and rest first, work afterward. Now it is more than work—it is conflict. And the mercy is more strikingly portrayed as being granted not only *before toil,* but *in warfare.* Life is a sore fight. But to the Christian man, in spite of all the tumult, life is a festal banquet. There stand the enemies, ringing around him with cruel eyes waiting to slip upon him like eager dogs around the poor beast of the chase. But for all that, here is spread a table in the wilderness, made ready by invisible hands. The grim-eyed foe is held back in the leash until the servant of God has fed and been strengthened. This is our condition—always the foe, always the table.

What sort of a meal should that be? The soldiers who eat and drink, and are drunken in the presence of the enemy, like the Saxons before Hastings, what will become of them? Drink the cup of gladness, as men do when their foe is at their side, looking askance over the rim with one hand on the sword ready, aye, ready, against treachery and surprise. But the presence of the danger should make the feast more enjoyable, too, by the moderation it enforces and by the contrast it affords—as to sailors on shore or soldiers in a truce. Joy may grow on the very face of danger, as a slender rosebush flings its bright sprays and fragrant blossoms over the lip of a cataract. It is not the wild mirth of men in a pestilence, with their "Let us eat and drink; for to morrow we die" (1 Cor. 15:32; see Isa. 22:13), but the simple-hearted gladness of those who have preserved the invaluable childhood gift of living in the present moment because they know that tomorrow will bring God, whatever it brings, and not take away His care and love, whatever it takes away.

This, then, is the form under which the experience of the past is presented in the second portion—joy in conflict, rest and food even in the strife. Upon that there is built a hope which transcends that in the previous portion of the psalm. As to this life, *"Goodness and mercy shall follow [us]."* This is more than, *I will fear no evil.* That said, sorrow is not evil if God be with us. This says, sorrow is mercy. The one is hope looking mainly at outward circumstances, the other is hope learning the spirit and meaning of them all. These two angels of God—goodness and mercy—shall follow and encamp around the pilgrim. The enemies whom God held back while he feasted may pursue but will not overtake him. They will be distanced sooner or later. But the white wings of these messengers of the covenant shall never be far away from the journeying child, and the air shall often be filled with the music of their comings. Their celestial weapons shall glance around him in all the fight, and their soft arms shall bear him up over all the rough ways, and up higher at last to the throne.

So much for the earthly future. But higher than all that rises the confidence of the closing words, *"I will dwell in the house of the Lord for ever."* This should be at once the crown of all our hopes for the future, and the one great lesson taught us by all the vicissitudes of life. The sorrows and the joys, the journeying and the rest, the temporary repose and the frequent struggles, all these should make us *sure* that there is an end that will interpret them all, to which they all point, for which they may all prepare. We get the table in the wilderness here. It is as when the son of some great king comes back from foreign soil to his father's dominions. He is welcomed at every stage in his journey to the capital with pomp of festival and messengers from the throne, until he enters at last his palace home. There the travel-stained robe is laid aside, and he sits down with his father at his table. God provides for us here in the presence of our enemies; it is wilderness food we get, manna from heaven, and water from the rock. We eat in haste, staff in hand, and standing around the meal. But yonder we sit down with the Shepherd, the Master of the house, at His table in His kingdom. We put off the pilgrim dress and put on the royal robe. We lay aside the sword and clasp the palm. Far off, and lost to sight, are all the enemies. We fear no change. We go no more out.

The sheep are led by many a way, sometimes through sweet meadows, sometimes limping along sharp-flinted dusty highways, sometimes high up over rough rocky mountain passes, sometimes down through deep gorges with no sunshine in their gloom. But they are ever being led to one place, and when the hot day is over they are gathered into one fold, and the sinking sun sees them safe, where no wolf can come, nor any robber climb up any more, but all shall rest forever under the Shepherd's eye.

Friends, can you take this psalm for yours? Have you returned to Christ, "the Shepherd and Bishop of your souls" (1 Peter 2:25)? Oh! let Him, the Shepherd of Israel, and the Lamb of God, one of the fold and yet the guide and defender of it, human and divine, bear you away from the dreary wilderness where He has come seeking you. He will carry you rejoicing to the fold, if only you will trust yourselves to His gentle arm. He will restore your soul. He will lead you and keep you from all dangers, guard you from every sin, strengthen you when you come to die, and bring you to the fair plains beyond that narrow gorge of frowning rock.

Then this sweet psalm shall receive its highest fulfillment, for then "they shall hunger no more, neither thirst any more; neither shall the sun light on them, nor any heat. For the Lamb which is in the midst of the throne shall feed them, and shall lead them unto living fountains of waters: and God shall wipe away all tears from their eyes" (Rev. 7:16–17).

The Good Shepherd

Henry Parry Liddon (1829–1890) belonged to the High Church school of the Anglican Church. Ordained in 1853, he served in two brief pastorates and as vice principal of a school. He moved to Oxford and there preached to large crowds at St. Mary's and Christ Church. He is perhaps best known for his Bampton Lectures, *The Divinity of Our Lord and Savior Jesus Christ.* From 1870 to his death, he was canon of St. Paul's Cathedral, London, which he sought to make into an Anglican preaching center to rival Charles Spurgeon's Metropolitan Tabernacle.

This sermon, slightly abridged, was taken from *Easter in St. Paul's,* published by Longmans, Green and Company, London, in 1907.

6

The Good Shepherd

[Jesus said], I am the good shepherd. (John 10:11)

PERHAPS NO ONE GOSPEL during the whole course of the church year speaks to us more directly, more persuasively, than that which is appointed for today. The Sunday of the Good Shepherd (i.e., the second Sunday after Easter), as in some parts of Christendom this day has been called, has an interest for us, "the sheep of his pasture" (Ps. 100:3), which need not be insisted on.

Three Distinct Allegories

In the first eighteen verses of the tenth chapter of John there are three distinct allegories. First comes the allegory of the Shepherd, next of the door, and lastly of the good or beautiful or ideal Shepherd. These, I say, are allegories rather than parables. An allegory differs from a parable as a transparency might differ from a painting on canvas. In the parable, the narrative has a body and substance, so to call it, of its own. It has a value that is independent of its application or interpretation. It often lends itself to more interpretations than one. In the allegory, the narrative suggests its one obvious interpretation step by step. Narrative and interpretation are practically inseparable.

It is impossible to look steadily at the picture presented to the mind's eye by the allegory without perceiving the real persons and events to which it refers, moving almost without disguise behind it. One illustration of this occurs in the allegory of Sarah and Hagar, which Paul interprets for us in the second lesson of this afternoon (Gal. 4:21–31). And another will be supplied as we proceed with the passage before us.

In order to understand the three allegories, we must remind ourselves that in the East a sheepfold is not a covered building but a simple enclosure of some extent surrounded by a wall or palisade. Within this enclosure are collected many flocks of sheep, which have wandered far and wide during the day under the care of shepherds. The shepherds head them to the enclosure or fold at nightfall, and during the night a single herdsman, here called the porter, keeps the gate and guarantees the safety of the collected flocks. In the morning the various shepherds return to the fold to claim their respective flocks from the hand of the night porter. They knock at the gate of the enclosure, and he lets them in. Then each for himself separates his own flock from the others with which during the night they have been intermixed. Each shepherd again leads his sheep forth to the day's pasturage.

Our Lord's three allegories place us face to face with the pastoral life of the East at three different periods of the Eastern day. In the first, the allegory of the *shepherd,* it is still the freshness of the early morning. The dew is on the ground, and the shepherds are returning to the fold to claim their flocks, which have been assembled within it during the night. If a robber endeavors to lead away some of the sheep, he must find entrance into the fold in some dishonorable way. He does not attempt the door, where he knows that he will be recognized and arrested. He climbs over some other part of the enclosure. He comes for no good purpose. He comes only to kill and to destroy. The porter only opens the gate to the regular shepherds. The shepherd calls his own sheep by name, and they know his voice. He leads them forth from the fold. He does not drive, he walks before them. They follow him because they know him and trust him.

The second allegory is that of the *door.* Here we are in the hot noontide of the Eastern day. The fold which is here implied, without being mentioned, is not that in which the sheep were collected during the night. It is a day enclosure to which, during the hours of burning sunshine, the sheep may retire for rest and shade, and out of which they may wander at will to seek for pasture. In this allegory there is no mention of a shepherd. He has disappeared. The most important feature is the door of the midday fold. The door of this fold is the guarantee of safety and of liberty to the sheep. "I am the door," says our Lord, "by me if any man enter in, he shall be saved, and shall go in and out, and find pasture" (John 10:9).

In the third allegory, that of the good shepherd, we have reached the evening. Already the shadows are lengthening upon the hills, and the shepherds have collected their flocks to lead them to the night enclosure. As the darkness gathers, the flock is attacked by wolves who lie in ambush for it. The good shepherd, who loves his sheep with a personal affection, throws himself between his imperiled flock and their cruel enemy, and in doing so sacrifices himself: "The good shepherd giveth his life for the sheep" (v. 11). This allegory of the good shepherd is not a mere repetition of the first allegory of the shepherd, although they both refer to one person and one only. The shepherd who knocks at the door in the early morning is contrasted with the thief and the robber who climbs into the fold some other way. The good shepherd who gives his life for his flock at nightfall is contrasted with the hireling or mercenary who flies at the approach of the wolf and sacrifices his flock for his own personal safety.

What to Understand by This Language

The question arises, "What would our Lord's hearers have been meant, in the first instance, to understand by this language?" And we must look for an answer in what was actually

going on at the time in Judea before the very eyes of the
Speaker. When our Lord spoke of a fold, every religious Jew
would think of the commonwealth or church of Israel. In the
pastoral language of the prophets the old theocratic nation was
the fold of the Lord Jehovah. When our Lord spoke of a shepherd, every religious Jew would think of the expected Messiah.
In the Twenty-third Psalm David applies the figure to the Lord
Jehovah as the guardian of his own life: "The LORD is my shepherd; I shall not want. He maketh me to lie down in green
pastures: he leadeth me beside the still waters" (Ps. 23:1–2).
But in Ezekiel 34:1–22 and Zechariah 11:3–12, Jehovah is announced as destined to appear once more to His people as the
Shepherd of Israel. In Zechariah, especially, the Shepherd of
Israel is represented as making a last effort to rescue the sacred flock from slaughter. But he only attaches to himself the
poorest of the flock, and after a month's toil receives thirty
pieces of silver, that is, the wages of a laborer of the lowest
class, as he breaks his staff and leaves the flock that will not be
saved from bad shepherds. The whole of this instructive but
difficult passage was, we may reverently conjecture, especially
before our Lord's mind when He was pronouncing these allegories. He was Himself, in His own thought, the Shepherd of
prophecy who had come to the gate of the Jewish commonwealth to discover and lead forth His own sheep.

But who was the porter? Among various explanations, there
is one answer that would have occurred to those who heard
our Lord and who knew the history of their own time, and it
cannot but occur to any careful student of John's gospel. The
porter is John the Baptist. It was to the Baptist, as last and greatest of the prophets keeping in the wilderness the gate of God's
ancient fold, that Christ came at the beginning of His ministry,
as the gospel dawn was breaking on the earth. It was from
among the Baptist's followers that Christ received His first disciples. "John bare witness of him" (John 1:15); this is the burden of the references to the Baptist in the last gospel. And who
were the thieves and robbers who had not come into the fold

through the gate? Preeminently, we cannot doubt, the Pharisees, who had established their great authority among the Jewish people by much hypocrisy and violence. They had not entered by the gate. Their influence was not based on the old Mosaic Law, but on bad traditions that had grown up around it and which they beyond others had fostered. And the Baptist, when he encountered them, as Matthew tells us, had not kept terms with them. They were a "generation of vipers . . . warned . . . to flee from the wrath to come [and to] bring forth therefore fruits meet for repentance" (Matt. 3:7–8).

The whole scene of the first allegory is laid at the commencement of Christ's ministry. In the second He has led out His own from the old Jewish fold into the pastures of the new kingdom. There is no shepherd mentioned here. Christ is the door. The new fold, of which He is the door, is the gospel enclosure, in which His person is everything. Through Him the sheep go forth for pasture and retire within for safety. Here again He contrasts Himself with the Pharisees as thieves and robbers. The image of the door melts away into His living person. In the third allegory, the last days of His ministry, which were already present when He was uttering these words, are before His mind. The evening is upon Him; He is near His passion. The wolf is lying in ambush for the flock. The hireling shepherd, true to his nature, flees; the Good Shepherd gives His life. Who is the wolf here? As always, the Pharisee party, which preyed upon the religious life of the people. Who is the hireling? Certainly not the Pharisee, against whom he is the natural defender. By the hireling, our Lord's hearers would have understood the Jewish priesthood.

It is a mistake to suppose that the interests and views of the Pharisees and of the priesthood were identical. The Pharisees were to a very great extent a lay sect. They had obtained a preponderating influence over the religious life of the Jewish people and had corrupted it very seriously. The priesthood ought to have held the Pharisees in check. They would have done so had they been faithful. The priesthood were not indisposed to believe in our Lord. In Stephen's day "a great company of the priests were obedient to the faith" (Acts 6:7). Even before the passion "the chief rulers . . . believed on [Jesus]; but because of the Pharisees they did not confess him, lest they should be put out of the synagogue" (John 12:42). The priests did not dare to resist the Pharisees, and Jesus was the victim of Pharisee indignation. It was already plain what would follow. Our Lord foreknew His sufferings, but an ordinary observer of the forces that were then governing the political life of Judea might have divined the meaning of the words, "I am the good shepherd: the good shepherd giveth his life for the sheep" (10:11).

Does the Title "the Good Shepherd" Still Have Meaning for Today?

When our Lord calls Himself the Good Shepherd, is He using a title which lost its value when He ceased to live visibly upon the earth? Or has this title any meaning for us Christians, for you and me, at the present day?

Here we cannot but observe that, writing some forty years after the Ascension, Peter calls Jesus Christ, as in today's epistle, "the Shepherd . . . of your souls" (1 Peter 2:25), and Paul calls Him "the great shepherd of the sheep" (Heb. 13:20).

In the earliest ages of the Christian church, when the stress of cruel persecution obliged the faithful and drove them from the public places of Rome to take refuge in the catacombs that were burrowed out beneath the crowded streets of the pagan city, there was one figure above all others that in their dark prison homes Christians delighted to sketch in rude outline on the vaults under which they prayed. It was the figure of the Good Shepherd. Sometimes His apostles were arranged on either side of Him. Sometimes the allegory was more closely adhered to and the sheep were standing around with upturned faces, eagerly intent upon their Deliverer and Guide. Sometimes, as more especially in later art, He was carrying a wanderer on His shoulder, or folding a lamb to His bosom, or gently leading the sick and weary of His flock. There was something in the figure which represented the tender and active care of our divine Master, moving, although unseen, among His persecuted flock to cheer and to save them. And ever since those days of persecution when Christ has been asked to bless a work of mercy for relieving the suffering, or teaching the ignorant, or delivering the captives, or raising the fallen, it has been as the Good Shepherd of the human race. The title has an attractive power that is all its own.

Not that it is easy for us at once to enter into the full meaning of this beautiful image. To do so we must know something about ourselves and something more about the person of our gracious Savior.

We must know our own weakness, our dependence, our need of a heavenly Guide and Friend. We must sincerely feel that, face to face with the eternal world and its awful Monarch, self-reliance, self-sufficiency is a fatal mistake. An old pagan Roman did not feel this. And therefore, in his unconverted state, he spurned the idea of having a Good Shepherd in heaven whom it was his business to love and worship. It was humiliating to him. It was intolerable that he, with the blood of the Scipios and the Caesars in his veins, should think and speak of himself as a sheep. To him the Christians who could do so appeared a set of poor-spirited, degraded, and contemptible people, who had never known what it was to have a part in the majesty of the Roman name. What did he want of a Shepherd in heaven? He depended on himself; he trusted himself. If life became intolerable, he probably meant to put an end to himself. That he should be led, pastured, folded, guarded, delivered—all this was out of the question. He did not want to be placed under a sense of obligation to anyone, least of all, under the sense of an obligation so utterly beyond discharge.

Certainly he might have reflected that he owed the gift of existence itself to some higher Being, and that this was a debt that he could never repay. But how many of us, Christians, go through life without ever seriously thinking what it is to have been created. What it is to have a Creator? What it is to have one Being to whose bounty all that we are and have, moment by moment, is due? What wonder if, like the old pagan Roman, we do not enter into the happiness of devotion to the Good Shepherd? Until the proud heart is broken by a sense of personal sin and by the love of God, revealed to the soul in His beauty and in His justice, the figure of the Good Shepherd would naturally be repulsive, as inflicting upon an ordinary man some sense of personal humiliation.

Moreover, if we would enter into what is meant by the Good Shepherd, we must know and believe the full and awful truth about the divine nature of Jesus Christ.

If Jesus Christ is merely a man, how could He be, in any rational sense, a Good Shepherd to you and me? It is now eighteen and a half centuries since He left the earth. And if we only think of Him as a departed saint resting somewhere in the bosom of God, we have no reason whatsoever to attribute to Him a pastoral interest in the multitude of Christians who look up to Him, day by day, hour by hour, for help and guidance. Can we suppose that any merely created being could thus be a superintending providence, an all-considering, all-embracing love to multitudes? Yet when our Lord says, "I am the good shepherd," He clearly disengages Himself from the historical incidents and the political circumstances that immediately surrounded Him. He places Himself above the narrowing conditions of time. He will be to all the ages what He is to the faithful few in and about Jerusalem. It is as when He says, "I am the light" (John 8:12), or "I am the way, the truth, and the life" (14:6), or "I am the resurrection, and the life" (11:25), or "I am the true vine" (15:1). All this language in the mouth of a merely human teacher would be pretentious, inflated, insufferable. We cannot conceive the best man we have ever known in life speaking of himself as the good shepherd of men. To do so would be to forfeit his claims to our love, our reverence, even to our respect. Why is it not so in our Lord? Because there is that in Him, beyond yet inseparable from His perfect manhood, which justifies His language. So that in Him it is not pretentious, not inflated, not absurd, not blasphemous, but, on the contrary, perfectly natural and obvious. We feel, in short, that He is divine. And such sayings as "Before Abraham was, I am" (John 8:58), "He that hath seen me hath seen the Father" (14:9), or "I and my Father are one" (10:30), are in the background. They explain and justify what He says about His being the ideal Shepherd of human souls. But it is because He is also man that such a title befits Him. Because He is no abstract providence but a divine person who has taken our human nature upon Him and who, through it, communicates with us and blesses us, He is the Good Shepherd of His people.

What This Truth Involves As to Our Relations with Our Blessed Savior

Let us reflect what this truth involves as to our relations with our blessed Savior.

As the Good Shepherd, He knows His sheep. He knows us; He knows us one by one; He knows all about each of us. "I am the good shepherd, and know my sheep" (John 10:14). He knows us, not merely as we seem to be, but as we are. Others look us in the face day by day, and we them. They touch the surface of our real life; perhaps they see a little way below the surface. But "what man knoweth the things of a man, save the spirit of man which is in him?" (1 Cor. 2:11). What do they know of that which passes in the inmost sanctuary of the reason, of the conscience, of the heart? Nothing. Do they know much of our outward circumstances, our trials, our struggles, our exceptional difficulties, or what we deem such? Citizens of this vast metropolis, we live amid a multitude while yet we are alone. But there is one Being who knows all, upon whom nothing that passes is lost, to whom nothing that affects us is a matter of indifference. To Him all hearts are open, all desires known. From Him no secrets are hid. All the warps of our self-love, all the depth and corruption of our hearts, all that we might have been, all that we are, is spread out as a map before

His eyes. Each moment that passes adds something which he has already anticipated. But yet the addition of new details forfeits nothing in the clearness of His comprehensive survey. It is because He knows us thus perfectly that He is able to help us, guide us, feed us, save us, if we will, even to the uttermost (Heb. 7:25).

While knowing us perfectly, the Good Shepherd has an entire sympathy with each of us. He is not a hard guardian who keeps us in order without understanding our difficulties. He is touched, as the apostle says, with a "feeling of our infirmities" (4:15). His true human nature is the seat and source of His perfect sympathy to which the image of a shepherd, if taken alone, would do less than perfect justice. Nothing that affects any of us is a matter of indifference to Him. He is not interested merely or chiefly in the noble, or the wealthy, or the intellectual, or the well bred. Wherever there is a human soul seeking the truth, a human heart longing to lavish its affection upon the eternal beauty, there He is at hand, unseen yet energetic, entering with perfect sympathy into every trial and anticipating, in ways we little dream of, every danger. He doesn't suspend our probation by putting us out of the way of temptation, but with each "temptation also mak[ing] a way to escape, that ye may be able to bear it" (1 Cor. 10:13).

For this sympathy is not a burst of unregulated affection. It is guided by perfect prudence, by the highest reason. In the days of His earthly ministry this was especially remarkable. He dealt with men according to their characters and capacities. He did not put "new cloth unto an old garment . . . [or] new wine into old bottles" (Matt. 9:16–17). He did not ask His disciples to imitate the austere life of the followers of the Baptist. He knew them too well. The days would come for that by and by. He did not at once unfold to them all the truth He had to tell about His own divine person, about His kingdom, about the means of living the new life. These truths would have shocked them, if prematurely announced. "I have yet many things to say unto you," He said, "but ye cannot bear them now.

Howbeit when he, the Spirit of truth, is come, he will guide you into all truth" (John 16:12–13). Those who were yet in the infancy of the Christian life were fed with milk. Strong meat was reserved for others who knew more and could bear more (Heb. 5:12–14).

So it has been ever since. If we have enjoyed opportunities, or have been denied them, this has not happened by chance. The Great Shepherd of the sheep has ordered it. He has proportioned our duties, our trials, our advantages, our drawbacks to our real needs—to our characters. We may have disputed His wisdom, or we may have made the most of it. But it is not the less certainly a characteristic of His government. "As thy days, so shall thy strength be" (Deut. 33:25) is a promise for all time.

Above all, as the Good Shepherd, Christ is disinterested. He gains nothing by watching, guarding, feeding us. He seeks not ours, but us. We can make no addition to His glory. He seeks us for our own sakes, not for His. He spent His earthly life among the villages and hamlets of a remote province when He might have illuminated and awed the intellectual centers of the world. He spared Himself no privations in His toil for souls. So absorbing was His labor that He had at times "no leisure so much as to eat" (Mark 6:31). Persecutions, humiliations, rebuffs, sufferings, could not diminish the ardor of His zeal. And He crowned all by voluntarily embracing an agonizing death in order to save His flock. Once for all, eighteen centuries ago, He gave His life for the sheep. But His death is just as powerful to deliver from the jaws of the wolf as it has ever been. Self-sacrifice, such as that on Calvary, does not lose its virtue with the lapse of years. The precious blood is today as powerful to save as, when warm and fresh, it ebbed forth from the wounds of the Crucified. For it is, as an apostle says, "the blood of the everlasting covenant" (Heb. 13:20).

The Great Shepherd of the sheep has been raised from the dead that He may plead for us perpetually in the courts of heaven. We look up to Him on His throne, and here in His temple we sing, day after day that "we are the people of his pasture, and the sheep of his hand" (Ps. 95:7). Do we mean it? We kneel day by day, and confess that we have erred and strayed from the eternal Father's ways, which are also His, "like lost sheep." Do we mean it? Have we yet returned to "the Shepherd and Bishop of [our] souls" (1 Peter 2:25). Do we endeavor to know Him as, whether we will or not, He certainly knows us? We need a Guide through the embarrassments of life. Do we recognize one in Him? We need a Physician for our moral wounds, a source of strength in our temptations, a rule and measure of holiness, an arm to lean on in "the valley of the shadow of death" (Ps. 23:4). All this He is and much more. But have we any practical knowledge of His being so? When He has fixed His eye upon us at some turning point of life, when He has reached out His shepherd's crook and beckoned us to follow Him, have we obeyed? No doubt faithfulness, submission, courage, perseverance were necessary on our part. But did He not merit these very graces for us? Has He done so much for us? Shall we do nothing—nothing—for Him?

Or if this has been with us as He would wish, are we now associating ourselves with his work? As we all may join in the intercessions of the Great High Priest, so we all may work under the guidance of the Good Shepherd. How many a work of mercy in the church of God has that gracious and tender figure inspired, which else had been denied to poor suffering human beings! By our individual exertions and by strengthening the hands and hearts of His ministers, by doing our best to raise their ideal and standard of work and life, by entering with sympathy and humility into cases of misery and ignorance which might well have been our own, we may all of us—laymen as well as pastors, women as well as men, simple and unlearned as well as lettered and wise—have a part in promoting among our fellows the knowledge of that redeeming love, which is the glory of our divine master Jesus and our own only ground of hope for time and eternity.

NOTES

The Lord's Guests

John Henry Jowett (1864–1923) was known as "the greatest preacher in the English-speaking world." He was born in Yorkshire, England. Ordained into the Congregational ministry, his second pastorate was at the famous Carr's Lane Church, Birmingham, where he followed the eminent Dr. Robert W. Dale. From 1911 to 1918, he pastored the Fifth Avenue Presbyterian Church, New York City; from 1918 to 1923, he ministered at Westminster Chapel, London, succeeding G. Campbell Morgan. Jowett wrote many books of devotional messages and sermons.

This message was taken from volume 5 of *Great Pulpit Masters,* published by the Fleming H. Revell Company in 1950.

7

The Lord's Guests

Thou preparest a table before me in the presence of mine enemies. (Psalm 23:5)

THIS IS A DESERT SCENE. A hot, panting fugitive is fleeing for his life, pursued and hunted by the forces of a fierce revenge. His crime is placarded on garments. The marks of blood are upon him. In a moment of passion, or in cool deliberateness, he has maimed and outraged his brother. And now fear has spurred him to flight. Nemesis is upon his track. He takes to the desert! The wild, inhospitable waste stretches before him in shadowless immensity. No bush offers him a secret shelter. No rock offers him a safe defense. He can almost feel the hot breath of his pursuers in the rear. Where shall he turn? His terrified eyes search the horizon, and in the cloudy distance he discerns the dim outlines of a desert tent. His excited nerves play like whips about his muscles, and with terrific strain he makes for the promised rest. The way is long! The enemy is near! The air is feverish! The night is falling! The runner is faint! Spurring himself anew and flinging all his wasting resources into the flight with the pursuers even at his heels, he stretches out toward the mark. And with one last tremendous exertion, he touches the tent rope and is safe!

He is now a guest of the desert man, and the guest is inviolable. All the hallowed sanctions of hospitality gather about him for his defense. He is taken into the tent and food is placed before him while his evaded pursuers stand frowningly at the door. The fugitive is at rest. If he can speak at all, I think his words will be these, "Thou preparest a table before me in the presence of mine enemies." Such is the undimmed glory of Arab hospitality. To injure a guest is the mark of the deepest depravity. Many of the Bedouins light fires in their encampments to guide the travelers or fugitives to their tents. Many of them keep dogs, not only for the purpose of watching against perils, but in order that by their bark they may guide the tired and benighted wayfarers to their place of rest. And so the fugitive finds food and shelter. To touch the tent rope is to enter the circle of inviolable hospitality. The host is the slave of the guest as long as the guest remains. All the resources of the tent are placed at his disposal. He can lie down in peace, and take his rest in safety. The pursuer is stayed beyond the tent. He can only "look" the revenge he dare not inflict. "Thou preparest a table before me in the presence of mine enemies."

Such is the desert symbol. What is its spiritual significance? The soul is a fugitive in flight across the plains of time. The soul is pursued by enemies, which disturb its peace and threaten its destruction. The soul is often terror-stricken. The soul is often a "haunt of fears." There are things it cannot escape, presences it cannot avoid, enemies that dog its track through the long, long day, from morning until night. What are these enemies that chase the soul across the ways of time? Can we name them?

Here is an enemy, the sin of yesterday. I cannot get away from it. When I have half-forgotten it and leave it slumbering in the rear, it is suddenly awake again, and, like a hound, it is baying at my heels. Some days are days of peculiar intensity, and the far-off experience draws near and assumes the vividness of an immediate act. Yesterday pursues today and threatens it!

> O! I have passed a miserable night,
> So full of ugly sights, of ghastly dreams,
> That, as I am a Christian faithful man,
> I would not spend another such a night,
> Though 'twere to buy a world of happy days,
> So full of dismal terror was the time.

And what were the "ugly sights" which filled the time with "dismal terror"? They were the threatening presences of old sins pursuing in full cry across the years! The affrighted experience is all foreshadowed by the Word of God. Whether I turn to the Old Testament or to the New Testament, the awful succession is proclaimed as a primary law of the spiritual life. "Evil pursueth sinners" (Prov. 13:21). That sounds significant of desert flight and hot pursuit. "Be sure your sin will find you out" (Num. 32:23), as though our sin were an objective reality. The hounds of Nemesis have found the scent, and they are following on in fierce pursuit! "Be Sure your sin will find you out." If I turn to the New Testament, the dark succession is made equally sure: "Their works do follow them." I know these words are spoken of the good, the spiritually-minded, the men, and the women who have spent themselves in beneficent sacrifice. "Their works do follow them" (Rev. 14:13). They are attended by the radiant procession of their services, a shining, singing throng, conducting them in jubilation along the ways of time into the temple of the blest! But the converse is equally true. The spiritually rebellious and unclean are followed by the dark and ugly procession of their own deeds, every deed a menacing foe, reaching out a condemnatory finger, and pursuing them through the portals of death into the very precincts of the judgment throne. "Their works do follow them." The sin of yesterday is chasing the soul across the plains of today! "Since thou hast not hated blood, even blood shall pursue thee" (Ezek. 35:6).

Here is another enemy, the temptation of today. Yesterday is not the only menacing presence; there is the insidious seducer who stands by the wayside today. Sometimes he approaches me in deceptive deliberateness; sometimes his advance is so stealthy that in a moment I am caught in his snare! At one time he comes near me like a fox; at other times he leaps upon me like a lion out of the thicket. At one time the menace is in my passions, and again it crouches very near my prayers! Now the enemy draws near in the heavy guise of carnality, "the lust of the flesh"; and now in the lighter robe of covetousness, "the lust of the eyes"; and now in the delicate garb of vanity, "the pride of life" (1 John 2:16). But in all the many guises it is the one foe. In the manifold suggestions there is one threat. "The enemy that sowed them is the devil" (Matt. 13:39). If I am awake, I fear! If I move, he follows! "When I would do good, evil is present with me" (Rom. 7:21). "O wretched man that I am! who shall deliver me from the body of this death?" (v. 24). The soul is in the desert, chased by the enemy of ever-present temptation.

Here is a third enemy, the death that awaits me tomorrow. "And I looked, and behold a pale horse: and his name that sat on him was Death, and Hell followed with him" (Rev. 6:8). Man seeks to banish that presence from his conscience, but he pathetically fails. The pale horse with his rider walks into our feasts! He forces himself into the wedding day! "To love and to cherish until death us do part!" We have almost agreed to exile his name from our vocabulary. If we are obliged to refer to him, we hide the slaughter-house under rose trees; we conceal the reality under more pleasing euphemisms. I have become insured. What for? Because tomorrow I may. . . . No, I do not speak in that wise. I banish the word at the threshold. I do not mention death or dying. How then? I have become insured, because "if anything should happen to me. . . ." In such circumlocution do I seek to evade the rider upon the pale horse. Yet the rider is getting nearer! Tomorrow he will dismount at the door, and his hand will be upon the latch! Shall we fear his pursuit? "The terrors of death are fallen upon me," cries the psalmist (Ps. 55:4). "Through fear of death they were all their lifetime subject to bondage," cries the apostle of the new covenant. It is an enemy we have got to meet. "The last enemy . . . is death" (1 Cor. 15:26). Here, then, we are, lone fugitives crossing the desert of time, chased by the sin of yesterday, menaced by the temptation of today, threatened by death tomorrow! The enemies are about us on every side. "My heart is sore pained within me: and the terrors of death are fallen upon me. Fearfulness and trembling are come upon me, and horror hath overwhelmed me. . . . Oh that I had wings like a dove! for then would I fly away and be at rest" (Ps. 55:4–6). Whither can we turn? On the whole vast plain, is there one tabernacle whose tent ropes we may touch, and in whose circle of hospitality we may find food and refuge and rest?

"God is our refuge and strength, a very present help in time of trouble" (Ps. 46:1). In the Lord our God is the fugitive's refuge. "In the secret of his tabernacle shall he hide me" (27:5). In the Lord our God we are secured against the destructiveness of our yesterdays, the menaces of today, and the darkening fears of the morrow. Our enemies are stayed at the door! We are the Lord's guests, and our sanctuary is inviolable! But what assurance have we that the Lord will take us in? I will give you the assurance. "Hath he said, and shall he not do it?" (Num. 23:19). I will give you the assurance. The most inspiring way to read the commandments of God is to interpret them also as evangels. Commandments are not only expressive of duties, they are revelations of God. Look into a commandment and you can see what you might be; look into a commandment and you will see what God is. Therefore, commandments are not only human ideals, they are expressive of divine glory. I would know, therefore, what the Lord has commanded in order that I may look into it for a vision of His face. He has commanded us to be "given to hospitality" (Rom. 12:13; 1 Tim. 3:2), to have the campfires lit that lost and fear-stricken pilgrims may be guided to shelter and rest. Then, are His campfires burning, and is He standing at the tent door to give the fugitives welcome? I have heard Him apportion the rewards of His kingdom and these were the terms of the benediction: "I was a stranger, and ye took me in" (Matt. 25:35). Then will the Lord Himself throw back the tent curtain, and take me out of the fright and darkness into the light and warmth and rest of His own abode!

> If I ask Him to receive me,
> Will He say me nay?
> Not till earth and not till heaven
> Pass away.

This, then, is my assurance. What He wants me to do, He does. What He empowers me to be, He is!

> Do I find love so full in my nature, God's ultimate gift,
> That I doubt His own love can compete with it? . . .
> Would I fain in my impotent yearning to do all for
> this man,
> And dare doubt He alone shall not help him, who yet
> alone can?
>
> . . . .
>
> Could I wrestle to raise him from sorrow, grow poor to
> enrich,
> To fill up his life, starve my own out, I would. . . .
> Would I suffer for him that I love? So wouldst Thou—
> so wilt Thou!

> I will flee unto Him to hide me.

And what shall I find in the tent? "Thou preparest a table before me in the presence of mine enemies." There is something so exuberantly triumphant in the psalmist's boast! It is laughingly defiant in its security. The enemies frown at the open door while he calmly sits down to a feast with his Lord. "Yesterday" glowers, but cannot hurt. "Today" tempts, but cannot entice. "Tomorrow" threatens, but cannot destroy. "O death, where is thy sting?" (1 Cor. 15:55). They are like the enemies which John Bunyan saw just outside the Valley of the Shadow, two giants by whose power and tyranny many had been cruelly put to death, but who can now "do little more than sit in the cave's mouth, grinning at pilgrims as they go by, and biting their nails because they cannot come at them." We taste our joys in the presence of our discomfited foe.

In "the secret of his tabernacle" (Ps. 27:5) we shall find a sure defense. "Who shall separate us from the love of Christ?" (Rom. 8:35). We shall find a refreshing repose. The shock of panic will be over. The waste of fear will be stayed. We shall "rest in the LORD" (Ps. 37:7), and "hide . . . under the shadow of thy wings" (17:8). We shall find an abundant provision. Our Host is grandly "given to hospitality." As quaint John Trapp says, "There is not only fulness, but redundance." He gives "good measure, pressed down, and shaken together, and running over" (Luke 6:38). On the Lord's table there is provision for everybody, and the nutriment is suited to each one's peculiar need.

The Divine Shepherd

Joseph Parker (1830–1902) was one of England's most popular preachers. Largely self-educated, Parker had pulpit gifts that soon moved him into leadership among the Congregationalists. He was a fearless and imaginative preacher who attracted both common people and the aristocracy, and he was particularly a "man's preacher." His *People's Bible* is a collection of the shorthand reports of the sermons and prayers that he delivered as he preached through the entire Bible in seven years (1884–1891). He pastored the Poultry Chapel, London, later called the City Temple, from 1869 until his death.

This sermon was taken from volume 12 of *The People's Bible*, published in 1900 by Hazell, Watson and Viney, London.

8

The Divine Shepherd

Psalm 23

THE LORD IS MY SHEPHERD; (v. 1)

It is vital that we should define God's relation to us, and our relation to God. Everyone may have an image peculiarly his own. An image that most clearly typifies the divine nearness and care, and through which, therefore, he can see most of God and understand Him best. God is the infinite name— Shepherd, Father, Healer, Deliverer. These are the incarnation of it, not in the sense of limiting it but in the sense of focalizing its glory and subduing it into daily use and daily comfort.

I shall not want. (v. 1)

An indirect tribute to the earthly shepherd. Some titles are characters as well as designations. A shepherd that allowed his flock to want would divest himself of his character, and rank himself with the horde of hirelings whose business it is to fleece the flock, and deliver it as a prey to the wolf. The assurance of nurture has here large meaning. It may be paraphrased variously: I am God's child, so I need not yield myself to anxiety; I am religious, therefore, I am provided for. Or the reasoning may start from the other and better point: God is for me, who can be against me? God is housekeeper, so there will be bread enough. God reigns, the universe is safe. There is no selfishness in the reasoning. The psalmist is not magnifying a little personality; he is stating the practical and universal sequence of fundamental reasoning. The violet is not immodest when it says in its mossy dell, "The sun shines, I shall be warmed."

> He maketh me to lie down in green pastures: he leadeth me beside the still waters. (v. 2)

He knows what I need. He treats me according to my quality. He proves by easily comprehended blessings that higher benefactions shall not be withheld. Pasture and water are the earnest and pledge of truth and grace. Did we know things as they are, we would know that they are all parables, whose meaning is spiritual. Bread is sacramental. Providence is the visible and historical aspect of theology. If God clothes the fields, will He not clothe the husbandmen? If He clothe the body, will He not clothe the soul? If He feed the flesh, will He starve the spirit? If we knew the earth aright, we should have some understanding of heaven.

> He restoreth my soul: he leadeth me in the paths of righteousness for his name's sake. (v. 3)

So the sweet singer has not missed the higher significance of his music. Already the green fields have lured him into the sanctuary; already the "waters of comfort" have brought him to the river of God. This is the very purpose of nature. All the stars lead to Bethlehem. All the waters trickle to the pure river of water of life, clear as crystal, proceeding out of the throne of God and of the Lamb. Oh that men were wise! then all nature would be but the vestibule of the sanctuary, and all providence but the many-figured gate that opens upon the soul's storehouse. Soul restoration is peculiarly the work of God. He alone knows that wonderful instrument, and He only can keep it in tune. "The inward man is renewed day by day" (2 Cor. 4:16). Day by day the soul must be judged, readjusted, fed, and comforted by the living One. The proof of renewal will be a steadfast walk in the paths of righteousness. Morality will prove religion. Sentiment will be crystallized in character. Is our piety rhapsody or service? Is our restoration a dream or a discipline? Do we know in our very heart of hearts that He who made the rainbow a covenant made the Cross the only way to heaven? These are the questions that shock the complacency of self-satisfaction, and bring men to penitence, confession, and prayer.

> Yea, though I walk through the valley of the shadow of death,
> I will fear no evil: (v. 4)

It is indeed the valley of shadows, the valley of night. However much the expression may be softened by Hebrew etymology and usage, we know what the valley is. It is ever before even the youngest life. It must be traversed, and the darkest part of it must be passed alone. Sweet mother cannot follow her child right through, and ardent love, the love which makes two souls one, must stand back in wonder and be made dumb with awe. Opinions come and go; laughter and madness have their times of riot and triumph; attention is arrested by politics, business, war, and pleasure. But there is the black, silent, gloomy valley waiting for us all! Is there no escape? May we not fly on white wings away to the city of light, the home of bliss? We know the answer. We bow our heads, and our hearts are cold with fear. "We must needs die" (2 Sam. 14:14). "There is no discharge in that war" (Eccl. 8:8). Proud, boastful, foolish man, let the "valley" sometimes come within your purview and sober you into a moment's considerateness!

> for thou art with me; thy rod and thy staff they comfort me.
> (v. 4)

Then the pious boast is not irrational, or presumptuous, or sentimental. It is a sanctuary built upon a rock. The psalmist will be without fear simply because he is in vital fellowship with God. Nor is he left with the overpowering thought of deity—a magnificent intellectual conception. He has something he can see and handle and enjoy, even a "rod" and a "staff." In many forms do these helps present themselves—the written Word, the palpable ordinance, the sympathetic friend, the remembered and realized promise—all those may be as the rod and staff of God meant for inspiration and comfort when the darkest cloud descends upon the expiring day. The peculiarity of the Christian religion is that it is most to us when we need it most. The night cannot frighten it; the storm has no effect upon its courage; death owns its sovereignty and retires before its approach. This is the sweet necessity of the case, for God can know no fear, and to be in God is to be like God. "Thou art with me"—my hand is locked in Yours, my life is drawn from Yours, my future is involved in Yours. God and the saint are one. When death triumphs, he slays not the saint only, but also God. Take heart, then, for this we know is impossible.

> Thou preparest a table before me in the presence of mine enemies: thou anointest my head with oil; my cup runneth over. (v. 5)

God is a hospitable host. He furnishes or spreads the table on a high mountain, and the enemy looks on with rage and impotence from the deep valley. God is the cup or portion of His people, and each can say, as in this case, "My cup is abundant—drink." God does everything for His people. Rod, staff, table, unction, cup, all are God's. "What hast thou that thou didst not receive?" (1 Cor. 4:7). Truly, my soul, God treats you as a favorite and sets on you special seals. So every believing man can say. Each of us seems to be God's only child—God's one ewe lamb—God's chosen delight. But all this favor involves corresponding responsibility. Nothing is said in mere words about the responsibility, but it is in the very heart and necessity of the case. We cannot receive all and return nothing. Gratitude must find its own most appropriate expressions. I must judge my piety as certainly by its gratitude as by its mercies. No gratitude means that the rain of love has been lost in a desert of insensibility.

> Surely goodness and mercy shall follow me all the days of my life: and I will dwell in the house of the LORD for ever. (v. 6)

It has been thought that this reference to the house of the Lord is decisive against the Davidic origin of the psalm. Perhaps so, in a purely literal sense, but certainly not in the larger interpretation of the singer's thought. The house of the Lord is a wide term. Jacob saw "the house of God" (Gen. 28:17) in an unexpected place. Surely there is a house for the heart—a sanctuary not made with hands—a hiding place and a covert from the storm. Is not this suggested by the very words "forever"? No man can literally abide in a literal house forever. Man dies, stone crumbles, all things earthly vanish as if but a phantasm. But this sweet singer says he will abide forever in a house that cannot be destroyed. The house of God is truth, wisdom, holiness, worship, sacrifice—it signifies nearness to God, communion with Him, a perpetual abiding under the shadow of the Almighty. My soul, seek no other home! In your Father's house there is bread enough and to spare, and they that trust Him shall want no good thing.

This sweetest psalm holds a place of its own in sacred minstrelsy. By many figures may its place be signified. It is the nightingale of poems, for it sings in the darkness of death's valley. Yet it is a poem that trills like the lark high above green pastures and landscapes, yellow with golden wheat. No, it is more than all this, for it seems to be sung by someone high in the summer light and, thus, to come down from heaven rather than rise from earth. Did some angel open heaven's gate and sing this lyric as the sun rose on the dewy pastures, and as morning made burnished silver of the tranquil streams? No—no. It is a human psalm. Even man may sing. Even sinners may celebrate "free grace and dying love." Sad is the psalmless heart—orphaned, indeed, and shepherdless is he who sits in silence when all nature celebrates the honor of her Lord. Shepherd of the universe, seek Your lost one!

NOTES

The Good Shepherd

John A. Broadus (1827–1895) has long been recognized as the "Dean of American teachers of homiletics." His work *The Preparation and Delivery of Sermons,* in its many revisions, has been a basic textbook for preachers since it was first published in 1870. Born and educated in Virginia, Broadus pastored the Baptist church at Charlottesville, and in 1859 became Professor of New Testament Interpretation and of Homiletics at the Southern Baptist Theological Seminary. He was named president of the school in 1888.

This sermon was taken from *Favorite Sermons of John A. Broadus,* published by Harper Brothers in 1959.

9

The Good Shepherd

I am the good shepherd. (John 10:11)

PASTORAL LIFE, ALWAYS MORE COMMON IN EAST THAN WEST, early became associated in men's minds and in literature with ideas of peace and tranquil enjoyment. Likewise, pastoral life has yielded many beautiful images to the inspired writers. But they used figures to teach spiritual truths. Many of the most famous men connected with the history of Israel were themselves shepherds.

Isaiah, looking forward to the Messiah amid the more splendid imagery with which he represents Him, touches our tenderest feelings when saying, "He shall feed his flock," and so forth (40:11).

So when Jesus came, He frequently availed Himself of this same image. He does not scrupulously adhere to the figure of a shepherd, nor need we. Consider Him.

I. As giving his life for the sheep.
1. He came, not as the thief [false teachers], but that they might have life (see John 10:10).
Imagine a flock, scattered, panic-struck because a furious lion has assailed them. But the shepherd comes and soon lies

dead in their defense; but the lion lies dead beside him, and the flock is safe. Heroic man, how he would be honored among the rustic people—his remains, his name. You see the parallel—so may angels honor our shepherd. But here the parallel ends—He died, yet He lives, to move among those He has died to save, to be loved and followed with new affection. He laid down His life that He might take it again.

2. He died voluntarily (see John 10:15, 18).

a. Disciples were likely to think, when so often told in advance and when His hour came, that men were compelling His death. In one sense this is true, in another it is purely voluntary. They could not, except He had chosen.

b. The Father did not compel Him to do it. Objection is sometimes made to atonement here—yet innocent not forced to suffer for guilty, it was voluntary.

c. But was it right that He should suffer, even voluntarily? He felt He had the right (see John 10:18).

We could never have asked Him to die for us. If it were now to be decided that He should be humiliated, suffer, and die to save us from destruction, every just and generous feeling would prompt us to say, "No. Let me bear what I have merited—let Him not suffer for me." Nonetheless, without our knowledge He did suffer and suffered out of love. Shall we reject Him? Now it is no longer a question, "Shall He die for us?" He did! "In his love and in his pity he redeemed [us]" (Isa. 63:9). Shall we accept the benefits secured by His dying love—shall we be grateful—love Him—be His? Consider

II. His tender care of His flock.

1. He knows them by name (see John 10:3). No danger that in the multitude anyone will be overlooked or forgotten. He knows every individual, and intimately.

2. He pursues the straying—"goeth into the mountains" (Matt. 18:12). This applied primarily to His coming into our world to seek and save the lost. Same thing is true of His gracious dealing with wanderers from His fold, backsliders.

Such wanderers should return to the Shepherd and Bishop of our souls (see 1 Peter 2:25).

3. He deals gently with recent and feeble believers, as is portrayed in the passage in Isaiah 40:11: "He shall gather the lambs with his arm, and carry them in his bosom." This does not refer to children particularly, as context would place beyond question, but to those who have recently become believers and are feeble. He will take care, shelter, bear along, strengthen. May your faith "groweth exceedingly" (2 Thess. 1:3). Now babes in Christ, you shall become perfect (full-grown) men in Christ Jesus.

4. He supports in danger and difficulty. The shadow of death is a highly poetical expression for the profoundest darkness. Conceive a flock led by the shepherd through a valley, deep, overshadowed, dark, where savage wild beasts abound, and yet they are fearless because the shepherd is with them. So we in seasons when, figuratively, our path lies through a dark valley, we will not fear because the Shepherd will be present. In affliction, when apt to feel deserted and desolate, He will be near, will uphold, and comfort. How beautiful, how delightful to a flock that has been passing through a dark valley will be the green pastures and quiet waters. And often when you have been afflicted, the subsequent seasons of health, prosperity, and tranquil happiness have been more delightful by reason of the shivering terror with which you had passed through that dark valley.

5. He guards in temptation. The flock, in a deep and dark valley, is especially exposed to wild beasts. So we have dreadful foes—"[our] adversary, the devil, as a roaring lion, walketh about, seeking whom he may devour" (1 Peter 5:8). The apostle here referred especially to persecution. The great enemy commonly comes against us. The Scripture has an expression more beautiful, and not less impressive: "Satan . . . transformed into an angel of light" (2 Cor. 11:14). Temptation has a dreadful power.

In the way a thousand snares
Lie to take us unawares;
Satan, with malicious art,
Watches each unguarded part;
But from Satan's malice free,
Saints shall soon victorious be;
Soon the joyful news will come,
"Child, your Father calls; come home."

6. He will continue to preserve them to the end (see John 10:27–29). This great truth is repeatedly and strongly taught in Scripture. If we become really His, He will not forsake us; we shall never cease to be His. The ground of this is in His power and unchangeableness—assurance of it is in His promises.

Some are afraid to undertake a life of piety, lest they should not hold out. Will the Savior hold out? He will give to us eternal life; we shall never perish.

Now how should the flock feel and act toward such a Shepherd? Only time for these things:

    a. Confide in His protecting care.

    b. Cherish toward Him a tender affection. The love of the flock for their Shepherd here a rebuke and a stimulation to us.

    c. Follow Him with unhesitating obedience.

NOTES

The Good Shepherd

Robert Murray McCheyne (1813–1843) is one of the brightest lights of the Church of Scotland. Born in Edinburgh, he was educated in Edinburgh and licensed to preach in 1835. For a brief time, he assisted his friend Andrew A. Bonar at Larbert and Duniplace. In 1836 he was ordained and installed as pastor of Saint Peter's Church, Dundee, where he served until his untimely death two months short of his thirtieth birthday. He was known for his personal sanctity and his penetrating ministry of the Word, and great crowds came to hear him preach. *The Memoirs of and Remains of Robert Murray McCheyne,* by Andrew Bonar, is a Christian classic that every minister of the gospel should read.

This sermon was taken from *Additional Remains of Robert Murray McCheyne,* published by William Oliphants and Company, Edinburgh, in 1846.

10

The Good Shepherd

John 10:1–6

WE MAY LEARN FROM JOHN 10:6 that this parable is difficult and dark to the natural eye: "They understood not what things they were which he spake unto them." How much need, then, have I of a fresh baptism of the Holy Spirit while I open it to you! And how much need have you to have the face of the covering destroyed from off your hearts and to receive the unction from the Holy One, that you may know all things!

1. The thief and robber.
2. The Good Shepherd.

The Thief and Robber

"Verily, verily, I say unto you, He that entereth not by the door into the sheepfold, . . . the same is a thief and a robber" (v. 1). There can be no doubt that this chapter is a continuation of the preceding. Jesus was showing the Pharisees what blind and guilty teachers they were. They were deeply offended at Him. In this chapter He goes on to show them the marks and defects of false teachers. It seems plain, however, that Jesus speaks mainly of one thief and robber. He calls him "a stranger" (v. 5), "the thief" (v. 10), "the hireling" (v. 13), and He contrasts him with the good shepherd, who gives his life for the sheep. Who is this thief and robber who climbs over the wall of the sheepfold? Who is this stranger who tries to lead away the sheep of Christ? Who is this thief and robber who comes not but for to kill, steal, and destroy? I have no doubt that it is Satan—the god of this world, the prince of the power of the air, he that entered into Judas, he who filled the heart of Ananias and Sapphira.

Satan has three ways of attacking the sheepfold.

Through Antichrist. There can be no doubt that Satan is the grand master-mover of all the workings of Antichrist. We are told so in 2 Thessalonians 2:8–9: "And then shall that Wicked be revealed, whom the Lord shall consume with the spirit of his mouth, and shall destroy with the brightness of his coming: Even him, whose coming is after the working of Satan with all power and signs and lying wonders." Again, Revelation 12:9: "And the great dragon was cast out, that old serpent, called the Devil, and Satan, which deceiveth the whole world." And again, Revelation 13:1–2: "And I stood upon the sand of the sea, and saw a beast rise up out of the sea, having seven heads and ten horns, and upon his horns ten crowns, and upon his heads the name of blasphemy. . . . and the dragon gave him his power, and his seat, and great authority." This is Satan's grand plan for killing and destroying the sheep of the sheepfold. Thus he wears out the saints of the Most High.

Through the world. Satan is the god of this world. From the days of Cain the world has come over the walls of the sheepfold to kill, steal, and destroy. The world, whether it smiles or frowns, hates the Christians and seeks to leap over the wall of the fold.

Through worldly ministers. Satan entered into Judas, and no doubt enters into many ministers still: "For such are false apostles, deceitful workers, transforming themselves into the apostles of Christ. And no marvel; for Satan himself is transformed into an angel of light" (2 Cor. 11:13–14). There is no way in which Satan has done more damage to the church than by thrusting unfaithful shepherds over the wall of the fold. Such were the Pharisees of old; such are careless ministers to this day.

The mark of the false shepherd: The false shepherd "entereth not by the door . . . but climbeth up some other way" (John 10:1). The door of the fold we know to be Christ: "I am the door: by me if any man enter in, he shall be saved" (v. 9). This is the sure mark of Satan and all his underlings—they do not enter in and are not saved through Christ. It is so with Satan himself. Unhappy spirit of evil, the strait gate of life was never opened to him. He leaps over the wall into the fold, seeking to devour the sheep—himself lost and unholy. So is it with Antichrist and all his ministers. They have never themselves entered by the door. They deny Christ to be the door. They would have men climb over some other way.

The object of the false shepherd: "The same is a thief and a robber. . . . The thief cometh not, but for to steal, and to kill, and to destroy" (vv. 1, 10). The object of Christ in coming to this world was to seek and to save that which was lost: "For the Son of man is not come to destroy men's lives, but to save them" (Luke 9:56). "I am come that they might have life, and that they might have it more abundantly" (John 10:10). So with all His ministers. Our heart's desire and prayer to God for you all is that you may be saved. We cease not from "warning every man, and teaching every man in all wisdom; that we may present every man perfect in Christ Jesus" (Col. 1:28). "I am made all things to all men, that I might by all means save some" (1 Cor. 9:22). But the object of Satan and all under him is "to steal, and to kill, and to destroy." First, *they seek to rob God.* Antichrist robs God of His throne, changing the very law of God. He robs Christ of the glory of being the only Mediator between God and man. The world robs God of His throne in your hearts. Worldly ministers rob God of His glory by concealing it, keeping back the counsel of God for man's salvation. The same are thieves and robbers. Second, *they seek to rob man.* Antichrist robs man of the Bible, of the preached gospel, of the way of

pardon and peace. The world tries to rob you of your peace—
of your way to holiness and eternal life. Worldly ministers seek
to rob you of your precious, never-dying souls.

Awake, my friends. You are in a dangerous time. Beware of
false shepherds, who come to you in sheep's clothing. Beware
of Antichrist, in whatever form he may come to you. Beware
of the world, whether in its frown or in its bewitching smile.
Beware of cold worldly ministers.

The Good Shepherd

The Shepherd of the sheep is the Lord Jesus Christ: "I am the good
shepherd" (John 10:11). "I am the good shepherd, and know
my sheep, and am known of mine (v. 14). Why does He get
this name? First, *because He died for the sheep.* He is not a thief
nor a robber, not a stranger nor a hireling, but the Shepherd
of the sheep: "All we like sheep have gone astray; we have
turned every one to his own way; and the LORD hath laid on
him the iniquity of us all" (Isa. 53:6). Second, *because He finds
the sheep:* "What man of you, having an hundred sheep, if he
lose one of them, doth not leave the ninety and nine in the
wilderness, and go after that which is lost, until he find it?"
(Luke 15:4). Every sheep in the fold has been found by Jesus.
Third, *because He carries the sheep:* "And when he hath found it,
he layeth it on his shoulders, rejoicing" (v. 5). He gathers the
lambs with His arm and carries them in His bosom. Fourth,
because He leads and feeds the sheep. They "go in and out, and
find pasture" (John 10:9). "The LORD is my shepherd; I shall
not want. He maketh me to lie down in green pastures: he
leadeth me beside the still waters" (Ps. 23:1–2). "For the Lamb
which is in the midst of the throne shall feed them, and shall
lend them unto living fountains of waters: and God shall wipe
away all tears from their eyes" (Rev. 7:17).

The marks of the good shepherd. First, *He entereth by the door.*
You may be surprised at this. Is not Christ Himself the door?
How can He enter by Himself? It was just by Himself that He
entered. Compare Hebrews 9:12, "By his own blood he entered

in once into the holy place," with 10:19–20, "Having therefore, brethren, boldness to enter into the holiest by the blood of Jesus, By a new and living way, which he hath consecrated for us, through the veil, that is to say, his flesh." Christ Himself entered in by this way to the Father, namely, by His own blood. By this way every faithful servant of Christ enters in: "He that entereth in by the door is the shepherd of the sheep" (John 10:2). O that God would raise up many such in Scotland—men who have entered in by the door into the sheepfold, and who can speak of sin because they have felt it and of pardon because it is sweet to them.

Second, *He calleth His own sheep by name.* In the Eastern countries, the shepherd frequently speaks to his sheep. He calls upon them, and they hear and know his voice. So is it with Christ. He is not a stranger shepherd nor a hireling; He calls His own sheep by name. This intimates, first, *His knowledge of them.* When Zacchaeus, a lost and wandering sheep, was straying far away from the fold, Jesus called him by his name: "Zacchaeus, . . . come down" (Luke 19:5). When Nathanael was wandering under the fig tree, Christ saw him and called him by his name. When Mary did not know Jesus, He said to her, *"Mary.* She turned herself, and saith unto him, Rabboni" (John 20:16). Christ knows all in this congregation who are His. He could name them over. He does often name them. Man does not know you, ministers do not, you may not know yourself; but Christ knows you: "He calleth his own sheep by name" (10:13). Second, *He deals in a very endearing manner with his own sheep.* This is implied. When you love a person, you love his name—it has music in it. So Christ loves to call His own sheep by name. He loves the name of those for whom He died. He holds sweet and daily communion with them. Third, *He changes their nature.* When Abram became a believer, Christ gave him a new name, so with Peter. So, when the Jews are brought to Christ, it is said, "Thou shalt be called by a new name, which the mouth of the Lord shall name" (Isa. 62:2). "But now thus saith the Lord that created thee, O Jacob, and he that formed thee, O

Israel, Fear not: for I have redeemed thee, I have called thee by thy name; thou art mine" (Isa. 43:1). "Him that overcometh will I make a pillar in the temple of my God, and he shall go no more out: and I will write upon him the name of my God, and the name of the city of my God, which is the New Jerusalem, which cometh down out of heaven from my God: and I will write upon him *my new name*" (Rev. 3:12).

If one of you were brought to Christ this day, you would get a new heart and a new name. You would no more be called worldling, swearer, drunkard, wanton but disciple, child of God, heir of glory, Christian indeed. Has Christ called you by your name?

He goeth before them. He did so while on earth. He went through all that He calls us to follow Him in. He went before us in faith and holiness. He went before us in labors of love—in reproaches, in necessities, in sufferings, in death. He does not ask you to go through anything that He did not go through. He still goes before His sheep, often unseen, often unfelt and unheeded, but still present. He will not leave you orphans: "When thou passest through the waters, I will be with thee; and through the rivers, they shall not overflow thee: when thou walkest through the fire, thou shalt not be burned; neither shall the flame kindle upon thee" (Isa. 43:2).

My dear friends, are you following Jesus, the Good Shepherd, or a stranger? Ah! flee from strangers. Flee from the company of the world, where you cannot hear the voice of Jesus. It is not safe to be there. Flee from those houses where the voice of Jesus is not heard, but the voice of strangers. Follow Jesus. Keep your eye on the Master. Believe on Him and do not let Him go.

The Good Shepherd

Henry (Harry) Allan Ironside (1878–1951) was born in Toronto, Canada, raised in California, and began preaching when he was converted at the age of fourteen. He had no formal training for the ministry but devoted himself to the reading and studying of the Bible. His early associations were with the Salvation Army, but then he identified with the Plymouth Brethren and became one of their most beloved itinerant Bible teachers. From 1930 to 1948, he pastored the Moody Church in Chicago. Ironside wrote more than sixty books, many of which are collections of messages given at Moody Church and various conferences.

This message was taken from *The Gospel of John Addresses,* a series of messages given at Moody Church and published by Loizeaux Brothers in 1974.

11

The Good Shepherd

John 10:1–16

WE REALLY HAVE TWO DISTINCT SECTIONS IN THIS PORTION. The first five verses constitute a complete parable in themselves, and then in verses six to sixteen we have added instruction and a fuller opening up of the truth of the shepherd character of our Lord Jesus Christ. He is emphatically the Good Shepherd. It is a rather significant thing that the word *good* here is one that really means "beautiful." "I am the beautiful Shepherd." Of course, it refers to beauty of character—the Shepherd who is absolutely unselfish and devoted to the will of the Father. He presented Himself to Israel as their Shepherd, and this was in accordance with many Old Testament messianic Scriptures. In Genesis 49, when by divine inspiration Jacob is speaking of Joseph, he concludes with these words, "Joseph is a fruitful bough, even a fruitful bough by a well; whose branches run over the wall: the archers have sorely grieved him, and shot at him, and hated him: but his bow abode in strength, and the arms of his hands were made strong by the hands of the mighty God of Jacob; (from there is the shepherd, the stone of Israel)" (vv. 22–24). That is, the Shepherd is from the mighty God of Jacob. He brings this in here because the experiences that the true

Shepherd, the Stone of Israel, was destined to pass through were so nearly akin to those that Joseph had to endure, rejected and spurned as he was, by his own brethren. Then we have the Messiah spoken of as Jehovah's Shepherd in Psalm 23, that beautiful gem which we love so much. Somebody has said that it is more loved and less believed than any other portion of Holy Scripture. "The LORD is my shepherd; I shall not want" (v. 1). We love to repeat the words, but how many believe them? How often we get panicky when the purse is empty and we are out of employment! There is one thing to do, and that is turn to Him and leave all with Him. "The LORD is my shepherd; I shall not want."

Then in Psalm 80:1, "Give ear, O Shepherd of Israel, thou that leadest Joseph like a flock; thou that dwellest between the cherubims, shine forth." The Shepherd of Israel was God Himself, who was watching over His people and some day was to come into the world in human form in order to guide them into blessing. Isaiah portrays Him in this way. In 40:10, "Behold, the Lord GOD will come with strong hand, and his arm shall rule for him: behold, his reward is with him, and his work before him. He shall feed his flock like a shepherd: he shall gather the lambs with his arm, and carry them in his bosom, and shall gently lead those that are with young." This was the prophecy of the coming to this scene of the Lord's Anointed, Israel's Messiah.

Then in Jeremiah 31—that great chapter that tells of God's everlasting interest in His people Israel—in verses 10–11 we read, "Hear the word of the LORD, O ye nations, and declare it in the isles afar off, and say, He that scattered Israel will gather him, and keep him, as a shepherd doth his flock. For the LORD hath redeemed Jacob, and ransomed him from the hand of him that was stronger than he." It was given to Ezekiel to confirm this, when in 34:12–15 he says, "As a shepherd seeketh out his flock in the day that he is among his sheep that are scattered; so will I seek out my sheep, and will deliver them out of all places where they have been scattered in the cloudy and dark day. And I will bring them out from the people, and gather them from the countries, and will bring them to their own land, and feed them upon the mountains of Israel by the rivers, and in all the inhabited places of the country. I will feed them in a good pasture, and upon the high mountains of Israel shall their fold be: there shall they lie in a good fold, and in a fat pasture shall they feed upon the mountains of Israel. I will feed my flock, and I will cause them to lie down, saith the Lord GOD."

We might turn to many other passages that depict the Lord as a shepherd, passages that were destined to have their fulfillment in the person of our Lord Jesus Christ. So when He stood in the midst of Israel and declared Himself to be the Good Shepherd, they should have understood at once, for they were familiar with the Old Testament. These passages had been in their hearts and minds down through the centuries. They were looking for the coming of Jehovah's Shepherd, and now Jesus appeared and said, "I am the good shepherd." We noticed sometime ago, when speaking on the "I AMS" of Christ, that that expression is really a definite, divine title. Jesus takes that incommunicable name of God and He says, "I am the good shepherd" (John 10:11).

He puts Himself in contrast with false shepherds who had appeared from time to time: "Verily, verily, I say unto you, He that entereth not by the door into the sheepfold, but climbeth up some other way, the same is a thief and a robber. But he that entereth in by the door is the shepherd of the sheep" (v. 1). I think these words are generally misapplied or given a wrong application. I do not mean that they are made to teach something that is false, but they are used contrary to what is taught in this particular verse. How often you hear people say, "If anyone tries to get into heaven in some other way than through Christ, he is a thief and a robber." But that is not what the Lord is speaking about here, at all. It is perfectly true that if you try to enter heaven by some other way than trusting the Lord Jesus Christ, you will be like a thief trying to break into a place to which you have no title, "For there is none other name under heaven given among men, whereby we must be saved" (Acts 4:12).

But that is not what the Savior is speaking of here. He is not talking about getting into heaven. Heaven is not the sheepfold. Judaism was the sheepfold, and in the half century before the appearing of our Lord Jesus Christ there were many who came pretending to be Messiahs, but they did not come in by the door—that is, according to Scripture. They tried to climb up some other way, and He berated them as thieves and robbers. Then in contrast, He speaks of Himself: "But he that entereth in by the door is the shepherd of the sheep" (John 10:2). He came in exact accord with the prophetic Word. His life was in exact accord with the predictions of Old Testament Scriptures. "To him the porter openeth; and the sheep hear his voice; and he calleth his own sheep by name, and leadeth them out" (v. 3). John the Baptist was the porter, who had been sent of God to announce the coming of the Messiah. He told of One whose shoe-latchet he was not worthy to unloose. To him Jesus came for baptism. John said, "O Master, I am not worthy to baptize You. I need rather to be baptized by You. You are the sinless One, and I am baptizing sinners. This is a baptism of repentance, and You have nothing of which to repent" (see Matt. 3:13–14). Jesus said, "Suffer it to be so now" (v. 15). And in His baptism He pledged Himself to fulfill every righteous demand of the throne of God to meet the need of sinners. As He came forth from the waters, a voice from the heavens declared, "This is my beloved Son, in whom I am well pleased" (v. 17). He had entered in by the door into the sheepfold. The porter had opened the way. And the Spirit of God, descending like a dove, abode upon Him, anointing Him as Messiah. That is what the word *Messiah* implies, "the Anointed One." He was anointed that day by the Spirit of God as the true Shepherd of the sheep.

So He entered in by the door, and there were those within the sheepfold who received Him. These were those who were really God's children. They had opened their hearts already to His truth, and when Jesus came they said, "Why, this is the

Savior for whom we have been looking!" "The sheep hear his voice; and he calleth his own sheep by name" (John 10:3). He did not intend to leave them forever in the fold of Judaism, but He was to lead them into the liberty of grace and blessing of Christianity. He entered into the Jewish sheepfold to lead His church outside of Judaism into the liberty of grace. "When he putteth forth his own sheep, he goeth before them, and the sheep follow him: for they know his voice" (v. 4). This is the supreme test. Somebody says, "Well, I think I am a Christian, but I do not see why Christ had to come into the world and die to save sinners. I do not understand." That proclaims a very sad fact. It says that you do not really know the Shepherd's voice. You have never taken your place before God as a repentant sinner and received Christ in simple faith. Those who do are born again, they receive eternal life, and with that new life is linked a new nature that causes them to delight in obedience to His voice. They know Him. They know the Shepherd's voice. They will not follow a stranger.

And so we are told, "This parable spake Jesus unto them; but they understood not what things they were which he spake unto them" (v. 6). They could not follow; their eyes were blinded. They did not apprehend the meaning of this beautiful little picture that He presented to them, so He went on to open up things more fully. "Then said Jesus unto them again, Verily, verily, I say unto you, I am the door of the sheep. All that ever came before me are thieves and robbers: but the sheep did not hear them. I am the door: by me if any man enter in, he shall be saved, and shall go in and out, and find pasture" (vv. 7–9).

Now He seems to change the figure here. Before He said, "I am the shepherd, and I entered in by the door." Now He says, "I am the door." Is it contradictory? Not at all. You may have heard a little incident told by Dr. Piazzi Smith. On one occasion he saw a shepherd leading his flock up the hill. He led them into the fold and made them comfortable, and then Dr. Smith said, "Do you leave the sheep in this fold all night?" "Yes."

"But aren't there wild beasts around?" "Yes." "Won't they try to get the sheep?" "Yes." "Well, you have no door here. How can you keep the wild beasts out?" But the Arab shepherd lay down on his side, and as he settled himself in that entry way, he looked up and smiled and said, "I am the door." You see, no wild beast could enter without awakening him, and no sheep would go out over his body.

So Jesus said, "I am the door. I am the One through whom My sheep enter into blessing and I am their guard and their guide." Then He says, "I am the door: by me if any man enter in, he shall be saved, and shall go in and out, and find pasture" (v. 9). Oh, that is what David meant when he said, "He maketh me to lie down in green pastures: he leadeth me beside the still waters" (Ps. 23:2). The shepherd takes care of the sheep and guides them to proper pastures where they are refreshed and fed. So our blessed Lord makes Himself responsible for those who put their trust in Him.

Now in contrast to Himself, there were false teachers and prophets who are only concerned about their own welfare. There have been such all down through the centuries and the Lord spoke of them in very strong language. "The thief cometh not, but for to steal, and to kill, and to destroy: I am come that they might have life, and that they might have it more abundantly" (John 10:10). He came to give eternal life to all who put their trust in Him. And if we are walking in fellowship with God we have that abundant life. A great many Christians have life, but they do not seem to have abundant life. I was in a home lately where there were two children. One was sickly and pale, while the other was so lively that he was a constant annoyance to the little sickly one. As I looked at them I thought. "Well, they are like Christians." There are a lot of Christians who have life; they have trusted Jesus as Savior, but they do not seem to count much for God—no testimony, no witness. And then there are others who are spiritually exuberant, bearing a great witness for the One who has redeemed them, radiant as they live in fellowship with the Lord.

First, Jesus says, "I am the good shepherd: the good shepherd giveth his life for the sheep" (v. 11). Then He declares, "I am the good shepherd, and know my sheep, and am known of mine" (v. 14). You see two sides of truth here. As the Good Shepherd He went to Calvary's cross and there laid down His life. There "he was wounded for our transgressions, he was bruised for our iniquities: . . . and with his stripes we are healed" (Isa. 53:5). Oh, that wonderful Shepherd!

> O Thou great all-gracious Shepherd,
>   Shedding for us Thy life's blood,
> Unto shame and death delivered,
>   All to bring us nigh to God.

Because, you see, there was no other way. In Gethsemane He prayed, "If it be possible, let this cup pass from me" (Matt. 26:39). That is, "If it is possible to save sinners by any other means than by My drinking of the cup of judgment, then make it manifest." But there was no other way, and so the Good Shepherd went out to die.

But He who died lives again. He lives in glory, and He is the Good Shepherd still. He is called elsewhere the Great Shepherd and the Chief Shepherd. "Our Lord Jesus, that great shepherd of the sheep . . . Make you perfect in every good work to do his will, working in you that which is wellpleasing in his sight, through Jesus Christ; to whom be glory for ever and ever" (Heb. 13:20–21). But this Great Shepherd is the Good Shepherd still. He knows His sheep, and He says, "I . . . am known of mine" (John 10:14). Does not that comfort your heart, dear child of God? If I am speaking to somebody who is lying on a sickbed—perhaps some of you have not been able to leave your bed for years, and the temptation would be to feel so utterly forsaken and lonely and tired and weary of it all—O dear, sick one, remember Jesus says, "I am the good shepherd, and know my sheep" (v. 14). He knows your struggles, disappointments, and the cup you have to drink. He drank a more bitter one Himself.

If in thy path some thorns are found,
  Oh, think who bore them on His brow!
If grief thy sorrowing heart hath found,
  It reached a holier than thou.

In His deep sympathy He enters into all your trials and shares all your griefs. And then—is it not blessed?—He says, "I . . . know my sheep, and am known of mine" (v. 14). And we say again with David, "The LORD is my shepherd; I shall not want" (Ps. 23:1). "As the Father knoweth me, so know I the Father: and I lay down my life for the sheep" (John 10:15). And, of course, He was speaking primarily of the sheep of the Jewish fold. But in the next verse we read, "And other sheep I have, which are not of this fold: them also I must bring, and they shall hear my voice; and there shall be one fold, and one shepherd" (v. 16). The word "fold" here should really be "flock." You see, Judaism was a fold, a circumference without a center, but Christianity is a flock where we have a center without a circumference. We have no wall about us, but we are gathered about Him, our Good Shepherd. Our Lord Jesus Christ is indeed our Good Shepherd, and "unto him shall the gathering of the peoples be" (Gen. 49:10).

NOTES

The Overflowing Cup

Charles Haddon Spurgeon (1834–1892) is undoubtedly the most famous minister of the nineteenth century. Converted in 1850, he united with the Baptists and soon began to preach in various places. He became pastor of the Baptist church in Waterbeach, England, in 1851, and three years later he was called to the decaying Park Street Church, London. Within a short time, the work began to prosper, a new church was built and dedicated in 1861, and Spurgeon became London's most popular preacher. In 1855, he began to publish his sermons weekly; today they make up the fifty-seven volumes of *The Metropolitan Tabernacle Pulpit*. He founded a pastor's college and several orphanages.

This sermon was taken from *The Metropolitan Tabernacle Pulpit*, volume 21.

12

The Overflowing Cup

My cup runneth over. (Psalm 23:5)

THE PSALM CULMINATES IN THIS EXPRESSION. The poet can mount no higher. He has endeavored to express the blessedness of his condition in having the Lord for his Shepherd, but after all his efforts he is conscious of failure. His sonnet has not reached the height of the great argument, nor has his soul, though enlarged with gratitude, been able to compass the immeasurable gifts of grace. Therefore, in holy wonder at the lavish superfluities of mercy he cries, "My cup runneth over." In one short but most expressive sentence he does as good as say, "Not only have I enough, but more than enough. I possess not only all that I am capable of containing, but I inherit an excess of joy, a redundancy of blessing, an extravagance of favor, a prodigality of love—'my cup runneth over.'"

We do not know when David wrote this psalm. There seems, however, to be no period of his life in which he could have used this expression in reference purely to his temporal circumstances. In his youth he was a shepherd boy and kept his father's flock. In such an occupation there were many hardships and discomforts, in addition to which he appears to have been the object of the ill-will of his brothers. He was not dandled on the knee of luxury nor pampered with indulgences. His was a hardy life abroad and a trying course at home. Unless he had been deeply spiritual and, therefore, found contentment in his God, he could not have said, "My cup runneth over." When he had come forth into public life, lived in the courts of Saul, and even had become the king's son-in-law, his position was far too perilous to afford him joy. The king hated him and sought his life many times. If it were not that he spoke of grace and not of outward circumstances, he could not then have said, "My cup runneth over." During the period of his exile, his haunts were in the dens and caves of the mountains and the lone places of the wilderness, which he fled for his life like a hunted partridge. He had no rest for the sole of his foot. His thirst after the ordinances of God's house was intense, and his companions were not such as to afford him solace. Surely it could only have been in reference to spiritual things that he could then have said, "My cup runneth over." When he came to be king over Israel, his circumstances, though far superior to any which he may have expected to reach, were very troublous ones for a long season. The house of Saul warred against him, and then the Philistines took up arms. He passed from war to war and marched from conflict to conflict. A king's position is in itself a thorny place, but this king had been a man of war from his youth up, so that, apart from the grace of God and the choice blessings of the covenant, he could not even on the throne have been able to say, "My cup runneth over."

In his later days, after his great sin with Bathsheba, his troubles were incessant and such as must have well nigh broken the old man's heart. You remember the cry, "O my son Absalom, my son, my son Absalom! would God I had died for thee, O Absalom, my son, my son!" (2 Sam. 18:33). That was the close of a long trial from his graceless favorite. A trial that had been preceded by many others, in which first one member of his family and then another departed from the paths of right. Nor did it close the chapter of his adversities, for the troubles of his heart were enlarged even to the last, and the good old man had to say upon his deathbed that, though he rejoiced in the sure covenant of God, yet his house was not so with God as his heart could have desired. We cannot, therefore, take the text and say, "This is the exclamation of a man in easy circumstances, who was never tried. This was the song of a favorite of providence, who never knew an ungratified wish." Not so. David was a man of troubles. He bore the yoke in his youth and was chastened in all his old age. You have before you not a Croesus whose long prosperity became itself a terror, nor an Alexander whose boundless conquests only excited new ambitions, nor even a Solomon whose reign was unbroken peace and commercial gain, but David, the man who cried, "Deep calleth unto deep at the noise of thy waterspouts: all thy waves and thy billows have gone over me" (Ps. 42:7). So did the spiritual outweigh the natural that the consolations of the son of Jesse exceeded his tribulation, and even in his most troublous times there were bright seasons of fellowship with the Lord in which he joyfully said, "My cup runneth over."

Let us think of *some cups that never run over.* Then consider, *if ours runs over, why it does so?* Then, thirdly, *what then?*

Cups That Never Run Over

Some men's cups never run over. Many even fail to be filled because *taken to the wrong source.* Such are the cups that are held beneath the drippings of the world's leaky cistern. Men try to find full satisfaction in wealth, but they never do. Pactolus fills no man's cup; that power belongs exclusively to the river whose streams make glad the city of God. As to money, every man will have enough when he has a little more, but contentment with his gains comes to no man. Wealth is not true riches, neither are men's hearts the fuller because their purses are heavy. Men have thought to fill their cups out of the foul pools of what they call "pleasure," but all in vain, for appetite grows, passion becomes voracious, and lust, like a horse leech, cries, "Give, give." Like the jaws of death and the maw of the sepulcher, the depraved heart can never be satisfied. At the polluted pool of pleasure no cup was ever yet filled though thousands have been broken. It is a corrosive liquor that eats into the pitcher and devours the vessel into which it flows.

Some have tried to fill their souls with fame. They have aspired to be great among their fellowmen and to wear honorable titles earned in war or gained in study. But satisfaction is not created by the highest renown. You shall turn to the biographies of the great and perceive that in their secret hearts they never gained contentment from the grandest successes they achieved. Perhaps, if you had to look out the truly miserable, you would do better to go to the Houses of Parliament and to the palaces of those who govern nations than to the purlieus of poverty, for awful misery is full often clothed in scarlet and agony feasts at the table of kings. From the sparkling founts of fame no cups are filled. Young man, you are just starting in life. You have the cup in your hand and want to fill it. Let us warn you (those of us who have tried the world) that it cannot fill your soul, not even with such poor sickly liquor as it offers you. It will pretend to fill, but fill it never can. There is a craving of the soul that can never be satisfied, except by its Creator. In God only is the fullness of the heart, which He has made for Himself.

Some cups are never filled, for the excellent reason that *the hearers of them suffer from the grievous disease of natural discontent.* All unconverted men are not equally discontented, but some are intensely so. You can no more fill the heart of a discontented man than you can fill a cup that has the bottom knocked out. A contented man may have enough, but a discontented man never can. His heart is like the Slough of Despond, into which thousands of wagon loads of the best material were cast, and yet the slough did swallow up all and was none the better. Discontent is a bottomless bog into which if one world were cast it would quiver and heave for another. A discontented man dooms himself to the direst form of poverty. Yes, he makes himself so great a pauper that the revenues of empires could not enrich him.

Are you the victims of discontent? Young men, do you feel

that you never can be contented while you are apprentices? Are you impatient in your present position? Believe me that, as George Herbert said of incomes in times gone by, "He that cannot live on twenty pounds a year cannot live on forty." So may I say: he who is not contented in his present position will not be contented in another though it brought him double possessions. If you were to accumulate property, young man, until you became enormously rich, yet, with that same hungry heart in your bosom you would still pine for more. When the vulture of dissatisfaction has once fixed its talons in the breast, it will not cease to tear at your vitals. Perhaps you are no longer under tutors and governors but have launched into life on your own account, and yet you are displeased with providence. You dreamed that if you were married, had your little ones about you, and a house all your own, then you would be satisfied. It has come to pass, but now scarcely anything contents you. The meal provided today was not good enough for you; the bed you will lie upon tonight will not be soft enough for you; the weather is too hot or too cold, too dry or too damp. You scarcely ever meet with one of your fellowmen who is quite to your mind. He is too sharp and rough-tempered, or else he is too easy and has "no spirit." Your type of a good man you never see. The great men are all dead, and the true men fail from this generation.

Some of you cannot be made happy. You are never right until everything is wrong nor bearable until you have had your morning's growl. There is no pleasing you. I know men who if they were in paradise would find fault with the glades of Eden, and would propose to turn the channels of its rivers and shift the position of its trees. If the serpent were excluded, they would demand liberty for him to enter and would grow indignant at his exclusion. They would criticize the music of the angels, find fault with the cherubim, and grow weary of white robes and harps of gold. Or, as a last resource, they would become angry with a place so completely blessed as not to afford them a corner for the indulgence of their spiteful censures. For such unrestful minds the cup that runs over is not prepared.

Some, too, we know whose cup never will run over because *they are envious*. They would be very well satisfied with what they have, but someone else has more and they cannot bear it. If they see another in a better position in society, they long to bring him down to their level. There are vices peculiar to the rich, but this is one of the ready faults of poverty. Now surely, friend, if you find your own lot hard to bear, you cannot wish another man to suffer it too. If your case be a hard one, you should be glad that others are not equally afflicted. It is a happy thing when a man gets rid of envy, for then he rejoices in the joy of others. With a secret appropriation which is far removed from anything like theft, he calls everything that belongs to other men his own, for he is rich in their riches, glad in their gladness, and, above all, happy that they are saved. Some of us have known what it is to doubt our own salvation and, yet, feel that we must always love Jesus Christ for saving other people. I charge you cast out envy! The green dragon is a very dangerous guest in any man's home.

Remember, it may lurk in the hearts of very good men. A preacher may not be able to appreciate the gifts of another preacher because they seem to be more attractive than his own. Good people when they see another useful are too much in the habit of saying, "Yes, but he does not do this," or, "She does not do that." The remark is made, "He is very useful but very crotchety," as if there ever was a man who did anything in this world that was not crotchety. Their very crotchets (which are uncomfortable things) God often overrules to be the power of the men and women whom He means to employ in striking out new paths of usefulness. What you call imprudence may be faith, and what you condemn as obstinacy may only be strength of mind needful for persevering under difficulties. Bless God for gracious men as you find them, and do not want them to be other than they are. When divine grace has renewed them, help them all you can and make the best use you can of them. If their bell does not ring out the same note as yours, and you cannot change its tone and, yet, feel that your note would be discordant to theirs, pray God to tune your bell to harmony with theirs that from the sacred steeple there may ring out a holy, hallowed, harmonious chime through the union of all the bells and all their tones in the sole praise of God. Envy prevents many cups from running over.

So, once more, in the best of men *unbelief is sure to prevent the cup running over.* You cannot get into the condition of the psalmist while you doubt your God. Note well how he puts it. "The LORD is my shepherd; I shall not want" (Ps. 23:1). He has no fears, forebodings, or doubts. He has given a writing of divorce between his soul and anxiety, and now he says, "My cup runneth over." What are you fretting about, my sister? What is the last new subject for worry? If you have fretted all your life, your husband, your children, and your servants have had a sad time of it. Your husband feels with regard to you, "Good woman, I know nothing in which I could find fault with her, except that she finds fault with others, and that she grieves when there is no cause for grieving." May the Lord be pleased to string your harp so that it may not give forth such jarring notes as it now does, but may yield the joyful music of praise. Your great need is a more childlike faith in God. Take God's Word, trust it, and, good sister, your cup will run over too.

What is your trouble, brother? You were smiling just now at the thought of how some women were troubled, for you thought, "Ah, they do not have the cares men have in business!" Little do you know. There is a burden for women to carry that is as heavy as that of their husbands and brothers. But what is your distress? Is it one that you dare not tell to God? Then what business have you with it? Is it one that you cannot tell to God? What is there in your heart that forbids your unburdening it? Is it one that you refuse to tell to God? Then it will be a trouble and a curse to you, and it will grow heavier and heavier until it will crush you to the earth. But, oh, come and tell your great Helper! You believe in God for your soul, believe in Him about your property; believe in God about your sick wife or your dying child; believe in God about your losses and bad debts and declining business. A bosom bare before the Lord is needful to perfect satisfaction.

I have proved God, and I speak what I do know. I have had a care that has troubled me, which I could scarcely communicate to another without, perhaps, making it worse. I have done my best and have prayed over it, but I have not seen a way of escape. At last I have left it with God, feeling that if He did not solve it, it must go unsolved. I have resolved that I would have nothing more to do with it, and when I have done that the difficulty has disappeared. In its disappearance I have found an additional reason for confidence in God and have been able again to say, "My cup runneth over."

We must walk by faith with both feet. Some try to walk by faith with the left foot, but their right foot they will not lift from the earth; therefore, they make no progress at all. Wholly by faith, wholly by faith must we live. He who learns to do that will soon say, "My cup runneth over."

I have not time to enlarge, although much more might be said, for there are cups that never have run over and never will.

If Our Cup Runs Over, Why Does It?

But now, secondly, why does our cup run over? Assuming that we have really believed in Jesus, and that not with a wavering faith but in downright solemn earnest, then joy will follow our faith. Our cup runs over, first, because, having Christ, *we have in Him all things.* "He that spared not his own Son, but delivered him up for us all, how shall he not with him also freely give us all things?" (Rom. 8:32).

> This world is ours, and worlds to come:
> Earth is our lodge, and heaven our home.

Between here and heaven there is nothing we shall want but what God has supplied. The promise is, "Seek ye first the kingdom of God, and his righteousness; and all these things shall be added unto you" (Matt. 6:33). As the old Puritan puts it, earthly comforts are like paper and string, which you need not go to buy for you will have them given to you when you purchase more valuable things. Seek the kingdom of God, and His righteousness, and all these things shall be added you. Our God is not like the Duke of Alva, who promised to spare the lives of certain Protestants and then denied them food so that they died of starvation. He does not give us eternal life and then deny us that which is needful to the securing of it. He will give us manna all the way from Goshen to Canaan and cause the gushing rock to follow us all the time we are in the wilderness. "No good thing will he withhold from them that walk uprightly" (Ps. 84:11). "Thy shoes shall be iron and brass; and as thy days, so shall thy strength be" (Deut. 33:25). I had climbed a hill the other day, and as I went down the steep side a sharp stone made a tremendous gash in my shoe. Then I thought of that promise, "Thy shoes shall be iron and brass." If the road be rough, a strong shoe shall fit the foot for it. As with the Israelites, their feet did not swell, neither did their garments wax old upon them, so shall it be with you (see Deut. 8:4). You shall find all things in God and God in all things.

But there is another reason why our cups run over. They run over *because the infinite God Himself is ours.* "The Lord is my shepherd." "My God," the psalmist styles Him. One of the most delightful renderings ever employed in a metrical translation of the Psalms is that of the old Scotch version of Psalm 42.

> For yet I know I shall him praise,
>   Who graciously to me
> The health is of my countenance;
>   Yea, *mine own God* is he.

I feel as if I could stop preaching and fall to repeating the words, "mine own God," "mine own God," for the Lord is as much my God as if there were no one else in the world to claim Him. Stand back angels and archangels, cherubim and seraphim, and all hosts redeemed by blood! Whatever may be your rights and privileges, you cannot lessen my inheritance. Assuredly, all of God is mine—all His fullness, all His attributes, all His love, all Himself. All is mine, for He has said, "I am thy God" (Isa. 41:10). What a portion is this! What mind can compass it? O, believer, see here your boundless treasure! Will not your cup run over now? What cup can hold your God? If your soul were enlarged and made as wide as heaven you could not hold your God. If you grew and grew and grew until your being were as vast as seven heavens, and the whole universe itself were dwarfed in comparison with your capacity, yet still you could not contain Him who is infinite. Truly, when you know by faith that Father, Son, and Spirit are all your own in covenant, your cup must run over.

But when do we feel this? When do we see that our cup runs over? I think it is first *when we receive a great deal more than we ever prayed for.* Has not that been your happy case? Mercy has come to your house, and you have said, "Whence is this to me? I never dared to seek so great a boon." "[He] . . . is able to do exceeding abundantly above all that we ask or think" (Eph. 3:20). You knelt down and prayed God to deliver you in trouble. He has done it. But instead of just barely carrying you through, He has set your feet in a large room, and you have said, "Is this the manner of man, O Lord God? Had You delivered me by the skin of my teeth I would have been grateful, but now my cup runs over." You asked the Lord to give you sufficient for the day, and, see, He has bestowed upon you a great many worldly comforts, and His blessing with them all. Must you not say, "My cup runneth over"? You asked Him to save your eldest daughter. But in His infinite mercy He has been pleased to convert several of your children, perhaps all. You began to teach in Sunday school, and you prayed to the Lord to give you one soul. Why, He has given you a score. Will you not say, "My cup runneth over"?

When I began to preach I am sure my little meeting house seemed large enough, and my sphere sufficiently extensive. If the Lord had said to me, "I will give you a thousand souls as your reward before you shall go to heaven," I should have been overjoyed and cried my eyes out with weeping for delight; but now how many thousands has He given me to be the seals of my ministry! My cup runs over! My God has dealt with me beyond all my expectations or desires! It is the way of Him! He gives like a king! He has outstripped my poor prayers and left my faith far in the rear. I am persuaded, beloved, that many of you know many things concerning God that you never asked to know, you possess covenant blessings that you never sought for, and you are in the enjoyment of attainments that you did not think it possible for you to gain, so that the cup of your prayer has been filled to the brim and it runs over. Glory be to the all-bounteous Lord.

So has it been with *the cup of our expectation,* for we ask many things and then from want of expecting them we fail to receive them. But have you not indulged large expectations, some of you? Have you not had your daydreams in which you pictured to yourself what a Christian might do? But the Lord has given you more than imagination pictured. You sat at mercy's gate and said, "Would God I might but enter to sit among the hired servants." But He has made you to sit at the table and killed for you the fatted calf. You were shivering in your rags and said, "Would God I might be washed from this filthiness, and my nakedness clothed a little!" But He has brought forth the best robe and put it on you. You said, "Oh, that I had a little joy and peace!" But He has made music and dancing for you, and your spirit rejoices abundantly in the God of your salvation. I will ask any Christian here if Christ is not a good Christ?

You know when Henry the Eighth married Anne of Cleves, Holbein was sent to paint her picture, with which the king was charmed. But when he saw the original, his judgment was very different, and he expressed disgust instead of affection. The painter had deceived him. Now, no such flatteries can ever be paid to our Lord Jesus Christ, the painters, I mean the preachers, all fall short. They have no faculty with which to set forth beauties so inexpressibly charming, so beyond all conception of mind and heart. The best things that have ever been sung by adoring poets, written by devout authors, or poured forth by seraphic preachers all fall below the surpassing excellence of our Redeemer. His living labors and His dying love have a value all their own. There are great surprises yet in store for those who know the Savior best. Jesus has filled the cup of our expectation until it runs over. And I may say the same of every mercy that He has brought in His hand. It has been a richer mercy, a rarer mercy, a more loving mercy, a more rapturous mercy, a fuller mercy, a more lasting mercy than ever we thought it possible for us to receive.

I speak to some who live by faith in their Lord's service. You have learned to expect great things, my brothers and sisters, and you will learn to expect greater things still. But has not God always kept pace with our expectation? Has He not outrun us? Has He not prevented us with His kindness? The path of a man who lives by faith is like a gigantic staircase. It winds up, up, up, in God's sight, into the clear crystal, but as far as we are concerned it seems to wind its way among dense clouds that are often dark as night. Every step we take we stand firmly on a slab of adamant, but we cannot see the next landing place for our foot. It looks as if we are about to plunge into an awful gulf, but we venture on and the next step is firm beneath our feet. We have ascended higher and higher. Yet the mysterious staircase still pierces the clouds, and we cannot see a step of the way. We have found our Jacob's ladder up to now to be firm as the everlasting hills, so we climb on. We mean to do so with the finger of God as our guide, His smile as our light, and His power as our support. The blessed voice is calling us, and our feet are borne upward by the summons, climbing on and on in the firm belief that when our flesh shall fail our soul shall find herself standing on the threshold of the new Jerusalem. Go on, beloved! God will do far more than you expect Him to do, and you shall sing, "My cup runneth over."

Sometimes, too, the text is true of the Christian's *joy*, "My cup runneth over." The other night as I sat among our young men in the ministry, and we were all singing, "I am so glad that Jesus loves me," I did not wonder that the writer of that piece made them repeat that delightful truth over and over again. "I am so glad that Jesus loves me." You can excuse monotonous repetitions and tautologies when that dear word is ringing in the ear: "Jesus loves me," "Jesus loves me," "Jesus loves me." Ring that bell again and yet again. What need of change when you have reached a perfect joy? Why ask for variety when you cannot conceive of anything more sweet? There is music both in the sound and the sense, and there is enough of weight, force, and power in the simple utterance of "Jesus loves me" to allow of its being repeated hundreds of times and, yet, never palling upon the ear.

Now and then I hear of an interruption of a sermon by a person who has found the Savior. How I wish we were often interrupted in that way! I wonder when men first learn that Jesus suffered in their stead that they do not shout and make the walls ring again. Surely it is enough to make them. What a blessing it would be if that old Methodist fire, which flamed so furiously in men's souls that they were forced to let the sparks fly up the chimney in hearty expressions, would but blaze away in our cold, formal assemblies. Come, let us pour out a libation of praise from our overflowing cups while we say again, "I am so glad that Jesus loves me." Have you not sat down when you have been alone and felt, "I am so happy because I am saved, forgiven, justified, a child of God, and am beloved of the Lord. This fills me with such joy that I can hardly contain myself"? Why, if anyone had come to you at such a time and said, "There is a legacy of ten thousand pounds left you." You would have snuffed at it and felt, "What is that? I have infinitely more than that, for I am a joint heir with Christ. My beloved is mine and I am His. 'My cup runneth over.' I have too much joy. 'I am so glad that Jesus loves me.'"

At such times *our gratitude ought to run over too.* Our poet's gratitude ran over when he wrote the remarkable stanza:

Through all eternity, to thee
My grateful song I'll raise;
But, oh, eternity's too short
To utter half thy praise.

I have heard cold critics condemn that verse, and therein prove their incompetence to enjoy poetry. Would they cramp the language of love by the rules of grammar? May not enthusiasm be allowed a language of its own? It is true it is incorrect to speak of eternity as "too short," but the inaccuracy is strictly accurate when love interprets it. When a cup runs over it does not drip, drip at so many drops a minute. It leaps down in its own disorderly fashion, and so does the grateful heart. Its utterances are as bold as it can make them, but they never satisfy itself. It labors to express itself in words, and sometimes it succeeds for a while and cries, "My heart is inditing a good matter. I speak of the things that I have made touching." But before long its rushing overflow stops up the channel of its utterance, and silence becomes both needful and refreshing. Our souls are sometimes cast into a swoon of happiness, wherein we rather live and breathe gratitude than feel any power to set it forth. As the lily and the rose praise God by pouring forth their lives in perfume, so do we feel an almost involuntary out gush of our very selves in love, which could by no artistic means tell forth itself. We are filled and overfilled, saturated, satiated with the divine sweetnesses.

Thy fulness, Lord, is mine, for oh!
That fulness is a fount as free
As it is inexhaustible;
Jehovah's boundless gift to me.
My Christ! O sing it in the heavens,
Let every angel lift his voice;
Sound with ten thousand harps his praise,
With me, ye heavenly hosts, rejoice!

What Then?

Now, thirdly, what then? The first thing is, *let us adore Him who has filled the cup.* If the cup runs over, let it run over upon the altar. "What shall I render unto the LORD for all his benefits toward me?" (Ps. 116:12). Remember, dear Christian friends, that preaching is not a result, it is a means to an end, and that end is the worship of God. The design of our solemn assemblies is adoration. That also is the aim and result of salvation, that the saved ones may fall down on their faces and worship the Lamb in His glory. Preaching and praying are like the stalks of the wheat, but hearty worship is the ear itself. If God has filled your cup, worship Him in the solemn silence of your soul. Let every power, passion, thought, emotion, ability, and capacity in lowest reverence adore the Lord of all, the Fountain whence flow the streams that have filled us to the brim.

The next thing is, if your cup runs over *pray the Lord to make it larger.* Does not the apostle say, "Be ye also enlarged" (2 Cor. 6:13)? Does not David speak of having his heart enlarged? There is too much of narrowness in the largest-hearted man. We are all but shallow vessels toward God. If we believed more and trusted more, we should have more, for the stint is not with God. Pray like Jabez of old, "Oh, that thou wouldest bless me indeed, and enlarge my coast" (1 Chron. 4:10).

The next thing is, if your cup is running over, *let it stop where it is.* Understand my meaning: the cup stands under the spring, and the spring keeps running into it. So the cup runs over, but it will not run over long if you take it from where the spring pours into it. The grateful heart runs over because the fountain of grace runs over. Keep your cup where it is. It is our unwisdom that we forsake the fountain of living waters and apply to the world's broken cisterns. We say in the old proverb, "Let well alone," but we forget this practical maxim with regard to the highest good. If your cup runs over, hear Christ say, "Abide in me" (John 15:4, 7). David had a mind to keep his cup where it was, and he said, "I will dwell in the house of the LORD for ever" (Ps. 23:6). When I preach abroad I always like to go to the same house in the town, and I say to my host, "I shall always come to you, as long as you invite me, for I do not think there is a better house." If a man has a good friend, it is a pity to change him—the older the friend the better. The bird that has a good nest had better keep to it. Gad not abroad, I charge you, but let the Lord be your dwelling place forever. Many have been fascinated by new notions and new doctrines. Every now and then somebody tells us he has found a wonderful diamond of new truth, but which generally turns out to be a piece of an old bottle. As for me, I want nothing new, for the old is better and my heart cries, "Return unto thy rest, O my soul; for the LORD hath dealt bountifully with thee" (Ps. 116:7). Until they find me a better fountain than the Lord has opened in Christ Jesus His Son, my soul will abide in her old place and plunge her pitcher into the living waters. Where my cup is filled there shall it stand and run over still.

Once more, does your cup run over? *Then call in your friends to get the overflow.* Let others participate in that which you do not wish to monopolize or intercept. Christian people ought to be like the cascades I have seen in brooks and rivers, always running over and so causing other falls, which again by their joyful excess cause fresh cascades and beauty is joyfully multiplied. Are not those fountains fair to look upon where the overflow of an upper basin causes the next to fall in a silver shower, and that again produces another glassy sheet of water? If God fills one of us, it is that we may bless others. If He gives His ministering servants sweet fellowship with Him, it is that their words may encourage others to seek the same fellowship. If their hearers get a portion of meat, it is that they may carry a portion home. If you get the water for your own mill and dam it up, you will find that it is overgrown with rank weeds and becomes a foul thing. Pull up the sluices, man, and let it run! There is nothing in the world better than circulation either for grace or for money. Let it run! There is more coming; there is more coming. To withhold will impoverish you; to scatter is to increase. If you get the joy of God in your heart, go and tell it to poor weeping Mary and doubting Thomas. It may be that God sent you the running over on purpose that those who were ready to perish might be refreshed.

Last of all, does your cup run over? Then *think of the fullness that resides in Him from whom it all proceeds.* Does your cup run over? Then think of the happiness that is in store for you when it always will run over in glory everlasting. Do you love the sunlight? Does it warm and cheer you? What must be to live in the sun, like the angel Uriel that Milton speaks of! Do you prize the love of Christ? Is it sweet to you? What will it be to bask in its unclouded light? Oh, that He would draw up the blinds that we might catch a glimpse of that face of His which is as the sun shining in His strength. What will it be to see His face and to enjoy the kisses of His mouth forever. The dew that distils from His hand makes the wilderness rejoice. What must it be to drink of the rivers of His pleasure? A crumb from His table has often made a banquet for His poor saints, but what will it be when the tree of life will yield them twelve manner of fruits, and they shall hunger no more? Bright days ought to remind our souls of heaven, only let us recollect that the brightest days below are not like the days of heaven any more than a day in a coal mine when the lamp burns most brightly can be compared to a summer's noon. Still, still, we are down below. The brightest joys of earth are only moonlight.

We shall get higher before long into the unclouded skies, into the land of which we read, "There shall be no night there" (Rev. 21:25; 22:5). How soon we shall be there none of us can tell! The angel beckons some of us. We hear the bells of heaven ringing in our ears even now. Very soon—so very soon—we cannot tell how very soon, we shall be with Jesus where He is and shall behold His glory. Friends, the thought of such amazing bliss makes our cups run over, and our happiness overflows as we remember that it will be forever, and forever, and forever. Eyes never to weep again, hands never to be soiled again, bones never to ache again, feet never to limp again, hearts never to be heavy again, but the whole man as full as it can be of delight ineffable, plunged into a sea of bliss, deluged within ecstatic joy, as full of heaven as heaven is full of Christ.

Dear hearer, the last word I have to say is this, do you know what it is to be filled with the love of God? Unconverted hearer, I know you are not happy. You say, "I wish my cup would run over!" What are you doing with it? "I am trying to empty it of my old sins." That will not make it run over. "I have been washing it with my tears." That will not make it run over. Do you know the only way of having joy and peace in your heart? What would you do with an empty cup if you were thirsty? Would you not hold it under a fountain until it was full? This is what you must do with your poor, dry, empty soul. Come and receive of Jesus, grace for grace. "But as many as received him, to them gave he power to become the sons of God, even to them that believe on his name" (John 1:12). Hold your empty cup under the stream of divine fullness, which flows to the guilty through Jesus Christ, and you also shall joyfully say, "My cup runneth over."